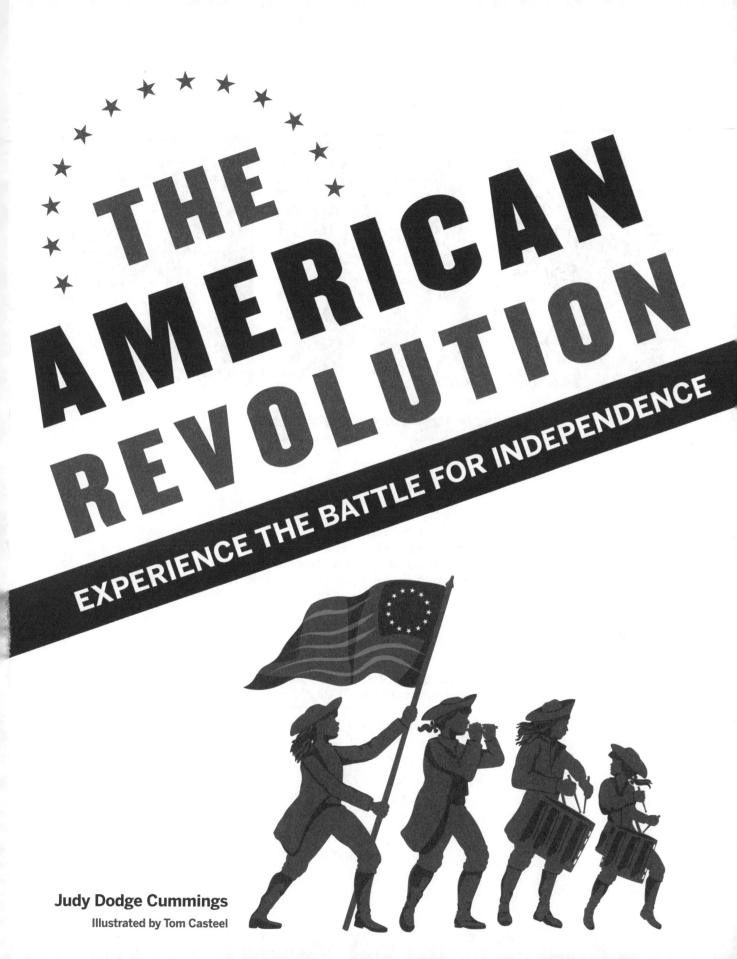

THE AMERICAN REVOLUTION

EXPERIENCE THE BATTLE FOR INDEPENDENCE

Judy Dodge Cummings

Illustrated by Tom Casteel

~ Latest titles in the *Build It Yourself* Series ~

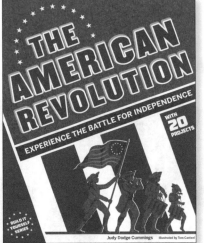

Check out more titles at www.nomadpress.net

Nomad Press
A division of Nomad Communications
10 9 8 7 6 5 4 3 2 1

This book was manufactured by Marquis Book Printing,
Montmagny, Québec, Canada
March 2015, Job #109665

ISBN Softcover: 978-1-61930-246-4
ISBN Hardcover: 978-1-61930-255-6

Illustrations by Tom Casteel
Educational Consultant, Marla Conn

Questions regarding the ordering of this book should be addressed to
Nomad Press
2456 Christian St.
White River Junction, VT 05001
www.nomadpress.net

Printed in Canada.

CONTENTS

Interested in primary sources?
Look for this icon.

PS

Use a smartphone or tablet app to scan the QR code and explore more about the American Revolution! You can find a list of URLs on the Resources page.

TIMELINE

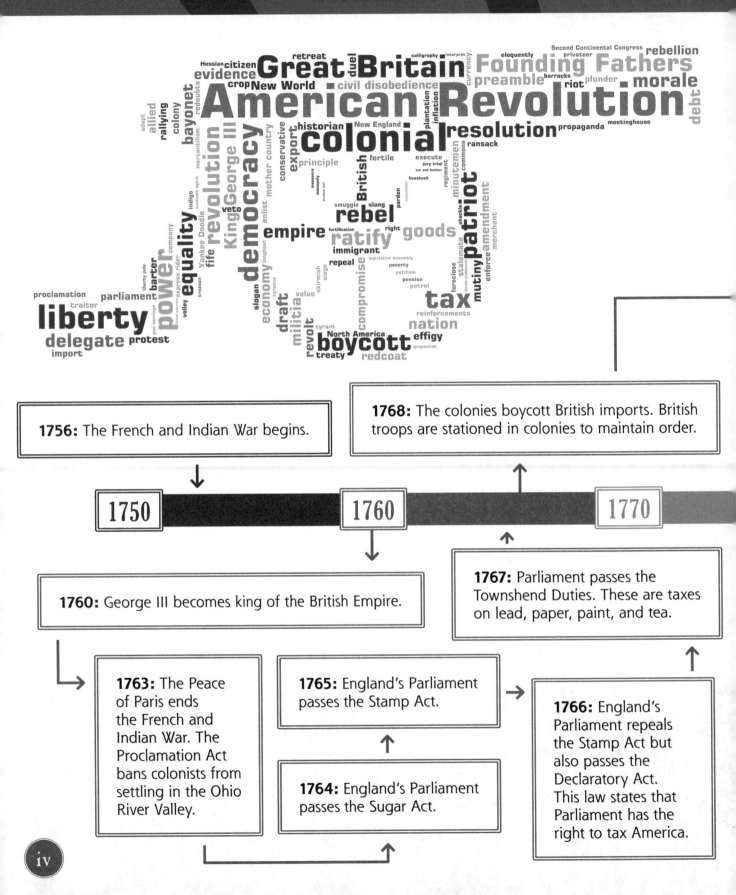

1756: The French and Indian War begins.

1768: The colonies boycott British imports. British troops are stationed in colonies to maintain order.

1750

1760

1770

1760: George III becomes king of the British Empire.

1767: Parliament passes the Townshend Duties. These are taxes on lead, paper, paint, and tea.

1763: The Peace of Paris ends the French and Indian War. The Proclamation Act bans colonists from settling in the Ohio River Valley.

1765: England's Parliament passes the Stamp Act.

1766: England's Parliament repeals the Stamp Act but also passes the Declaratory Act. This law states that Parliament has the right to tax America.

1764: England's Parliament passes the Sugar Act.

TIMELINE

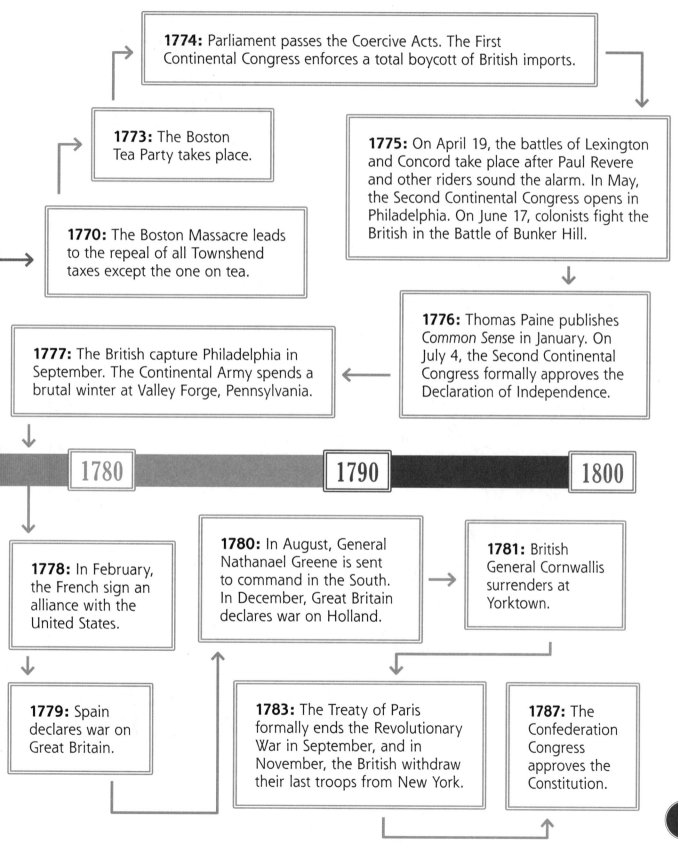

1774: Parliament passes the Coercive Acts. The First Continental Congress enforces a total boycott of British imports.

1773: The Boston Tea Party takes place.

1770: The Boston Massacre leads to the repeal of all Townshend taxes except the one on tea.

1775: On April 19, the battles of Lexington and Concord take place after Paul Revere and other riders sound the alarm. In May, the Second Continental Congress opens in Philadelphia. On June 17, colonists fight the British in the Battle of Bunker Hill.

1776: Thomas Paine publishes *Common Sense* in January. On July 4, the Second Continental Congress formally approves the Declaration of Independence.

1777: The British capture Philadelphia in September. The Continental Army spends a brutal winter at Valley Forge, Pennsylvania.

1780   1790   1800

1778: In February, the French sign an alliance with the United States.

1780: In August, General Nathanael Greene is sent to command in the South. In December, Great Britain declares war on Holland.

1781: British General Cornwallis surrenders at Yorktown.

1779: Spain declares war on Great Britain.

1783: The Treaty of Paris formally ends the Revolutionary War in September, and in November, the British withdraw their last troops from New York.

1787: The Confederation Congress approves the Constitution.

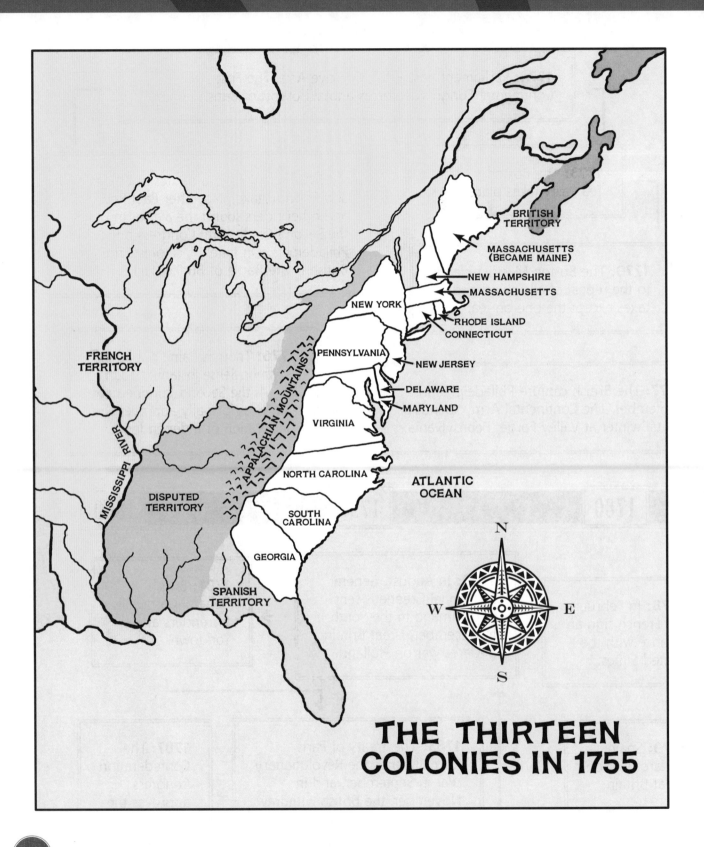

THE THIRTEEN
COLONIES IN 1755

BRITISH
TERRITORY

MASSACHUSETTS
(BECAME MAINE)

NEW HAMPSHIRE

MASSACHUSETTS

RHODE ISLAND

CONNECTICUT

NEW YORK

PENNSYLVANIA

NEW JERSEY

DELAWARE

MARYLAND

FRENCH
TERRITORY

VIRGINIA

NORTH CAROLINA

ATLANTIC
OCEAN

DISPUTED
TERRITORY

SOUTH
CAROLINA

GEORGIA

SPANISH
TERRITORY

MISSISSIPPI RIVER

APPALACHIAN MOUNTAINS

N

W   E

S

The Birth of a Nation

On July 4th, red, white, and blue flags wave in the wind. Drums beat a rat-a-tat-tat. Fireworks ignite the sky. Each year on this summer day, Americans celebrate the birthday of the United States. Do you know the real story behind the fireworks and fun?

revolution: an attempt to overthrow a government and replace it with a new system.

American Revolution: the war between the colonies and England from 1775 to 1783 that ended with the creation of the independent United States of America.

North America: the continent that includes the United States, Canada, Mexico, and all of the countries of Central America and the Caribbean.

British: citizens of the kingdom of Great Britain, which consisted of England, Scotland, and Wales.

citizen: a person who has all the rights and responsibilities that come with being a full member of a country.

colony: a territory controlled by another country.

mother country: the country that a person or group of people comes from.

nation: another word for country.

WORDS TO KNOW

The United States grew out of the ashes of **revolution**. This war, called the **American Revolution** or the Revolutionary War, was fought on the land between the Atlantic Ocean and the Mississippi River. Many people wanted to own this section of **North America**, which Native Americans first called home. The Spanish, the French, the Dutch, and, finally, the **British** all tried to settle this land.

The British settled 13 **colonies** along the Atlantic Coast, clearing the land and building towns and cities. But after a century, many British colonists, who lived in the colonies, began to resent the way their **mother country** of Great Britain ruled them.

In 1776, the colonists decided the time had come to rule themselves. They declared that they were the independent **nation** of the United States of America.

The British government refused to let the American colonies go without a fight, and so the Revolutionary War began.

Map It!

Look at this 1755 map of what is now the eastern United States.

How does it look different from today's map? This map was drawn by someone from Great Britain. Do you think it would look different if someone from France had made it? What about a colonist?

2

What caused the colonists to want to separate from Great Britain in 1776? What hardships did **colonial** families face when their farms became battlefields? How did the outnumbered and undersupplied colonial army defeat the British, which was the strongest **power** in the world?

As you read this book, you'll become an amateur **historian**. Historians ask questions and dig into the past to find the answers.

Prepare to be amazed, puzzled, disgusted, entertained, and intrigued as you follow the winding path of the colonists during the Revolutionary War.

DID YOU KNOW?

Americans have been celebrating the Fourth of July with fireworks since the very first Independence Day celebration in 1777.

Start a Historical Detective Journal

Each chapter of this book begins with an essential question to help guide your exploration of the American Revolution.

? ESSENTIAL QUESTION

Keep the question in your mind as you read the chapter. At the end of each chapter, **interpret** what you read and write a **thesis statement** to answer your question. Choose a spiral-bound notebook and label the cover "Historical Detective Journal." Use your journal to record your questions and answers about the Revolutionary War.

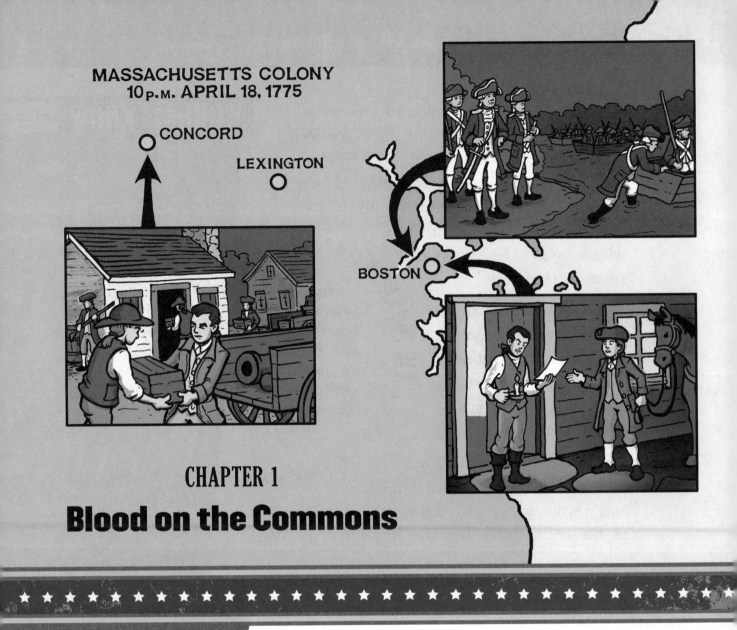

MASSACHUSETTS COLONY
10 P.M. APRIL 18, 1775

CONCORD

LEXINGTON

BOSTON

CHAPTER 1

Blood on the Commons

gun carriage: the platform
that carries a cannon.

meetinghouse: a building
used for public meetings
and as a church.

WORDS TO KNOW

gun carriage: the platform
that carries a cannon.

meetinghouse: a building
used for public meetings
and as a church.

On April 18, 1775, at 10 p.m. an
uneasy darkness cloaked the town
of Concord, Massachusetts. Cannon
parts had been hurriedly buried in the
cornfields. Gun carriages were hidden in the
meetinghouse and ammunition was stowed
in homes and taverns. The townspeople
of Concord knew the British Army would come hunting
for these weapons. They just didn't know when.

? **ESSENTIAL QUESTION**

Who was responsible for the violence that occurred in Massachusetts on April 19, 1775? Would the revolution have still happened if the outcome of this first battle had been different?

Meanwhile, in Boston, a heavy knock sounded on Paul Revere's door. When he opened it, a messenger handed him a note from Joseph Warren. Warren and Revere were members of the Committee of Safety.

All 13 American colonies had formed these committees. People were angry about the harsh way Great Britain was treating them, including charging high **taxes** and stationing British soldiers in cities. What was next? Colonists formed safety committees to train local **militia**.

They wanted to be able to defend themselves against the British Army.

Revere read Warren's message. Hundreds of British soldiers were marching from Boston to the towns of Lexington and Concord. The soldiers' mission was to arrest **patriot** leaders hiding in Lexington. They also planned to seize the weapons the colonists had stored in Concord. The time had come for Paul Revere and the other **express riders** to sound the alarm—the British were coming!

tax: an extra charge the government adds to the price of **goods** and services.

goods: items that can be bought, sold, or traded.

militia: an army made up of citizens instead of professional soldiers.

patriot: in colonial America, someone who resisted British rule. The British called these people **rebels**.

rebel: someone fighting against authority.

express rider: someone who carried messages from town to town on horseback.

WORDS TO KNOW

WORDS TO KNOW

longboat: a large boat used to carry soldiers from ship to shore.

King George III: the leader of Great Britain.

protest: to object to something, often in public.

rebellion: an organized attempt to overthrow a government or other authority.

revolt: to fight against a government or person of authority.

patrol: to keep watch over an area.

redcoat: slang for British soldiers, whose uniforms included red jackets.

slang: a nickname for something, used mostly in speech.

From a marshy area on the west side of Boston, British General Thomas Gage watched his soldiers cross Back Bay to Cambridge in a fleet of **longboats**. A few days earlier, Gage had received a top-secret command from authorities in England. The colonists of Massachusetts were refusing to pay taxes to **King George III**. They had thrown millions of dollars' worth of British tea into Boston Harbor in **protest**. This **rebellion** must be crushed!

*If the British army could capture the colonists' weapons, the colonists could not **revolt**.*

Gage's spies said the rebels had hidden weapons and ammunition in Concord, so the general sealed the road out of Boston. He posted watchmen on ships anchored in the Charles River and sent 20 officers to **patrol** the road west of Boston.

Late into the night, longboats carried the **redcoats** across Back Bay. The men shivered in the cold spring wind. Finally, around 2 a.m. on April 19, all the soldiers were on solid ground. The column of 900 British soldiers began the 13-mile march to Lexington. But by then, the countryside of Massachusetts was wide awake.

PS Sound the Alarm

Paul Revere's midnight ride is a famous moment in history. **Read his own description of his ride.** Is it different from what you've heard before? How? How is his language different from what we use today?

Midnight Riders

Long before the redcoats landed in Cambridge, Paul Revere was on his way. Friends rowed him across the Charles River to Charlestown. There, a man told Revere that he had spotted two lanterns in the tower of the Old North Church.

This was the signal that British troops were leaving Boston by water, not the land route. Another man loaned Revere his horse, Brown Beauty. In a long jacket, riding boots, and silver spurs, Paul Revere galloped for Lexington.

At midnight, he arrived at the home of Reverend Jonas Clarke in Lexington. Brown Beauty's mouth was lathered with foam from her hard ride and her flanks were bloody from Revere's spurs. A sergeant was guarding the door. He told Revere to hush.

DID YOU KNOW?

★ Paul Revere was a dentist as well as a silversmith. He was the first person to identify a dead body by looking at the teeth. ★

"Noise!" Revere exclaimed. "You'll have noise enough before long! The regulars are coming out!" The colonists often called the British "regulars."

Inside Reverend Clarke's home hid two of the men on Britain's most-wanted list: Samuel Adams and John Hancock. They were patriot leaders. For the past year, they had been organizing resistance to British laws that they believed were unfair to the colonists. If the British arrested them, Adams and Hancock would probably be **executed**. Paul Revere warned them that trouble was on the way.

WORDS TO KNOW

execute: to put to death.

7

Hancock polished his sword and cleaned his pistol. He wanted to stay and fight. Adams slapped Hancock on the shoulder and said, "Fighting is not our business. We belong in the cabinet [government]." Hancock gave in and they rode away in a carriage—the pair had slipped through the British net once again.

By this time, another express rider named William Dawes had arrived in Lexington. Joseph Warren had ordered him to take a different route from Boston. Revere and Dawes rode toward Concord to spread the alarm.

Samuel Prescott was in Lexington visiting his sweetheart. Her brother told Prescott about Revere's warning. Prescott jumped on his horse and galloped until he caught up to Dawes and Revere on the edge of Lexington. The three men joined forces.

Suddenly, when the riders were about halfway to Concord, four British soldiers emerged from the darkness on horseback. They drew their guns and threatened to shoot anyone who moved.

As the soldiers herded their prisoners toward a field, the men made a run for it. Prescott jumped his horse over a stone wall and disappeared into the night. Dawes's horse galloped between some buildings, but then tossed Dawes and ran away. Dawes had to limp back to Lexington.

Revere was quickly surrounded by the soldiers who threatened to "blow his brains out." Revere told the soldiers that 500 militia waited for them at Lexington. The worried soldiers ditched their prisoner, took Brown Beauty, and rode off to alert the British Army. Revere walked back to Lexington. He reached town at three o'clock in the morning.

The Midnight Ride of Paul Revere

In 1860, Henry Wadsworth Longfellow wrote a poem titled *Paul Revere's Ride*. The poem opens like a good story.

> *Listen my children and you shall hear,*
>
> *of the midnight ride of Paul Revere . . . .*

Stanza by stanza, the poem traces the night of April 18, 1775. Revere spies the lantern signal in the Old North Church. He rides to Lexington, then on to Concord and then keeps on going. The poem ends in a way that stirs the reader's heart.

> *For, borne on the night-wind of the Past,*
>
> *Through all our history, to the last,*
>
> *In the hour of darkness and peril and need,*
>
> *The people will waken and listen to hear*
>
> *The hurrying hoof-beats of that steed,*
>
> *And the midnight message of Paul Revere.*

Longfellow's poem made Paul Revere an American hero, but much of the poem is not historically **accurate**. Longfellow made up facts to fit the story he wanted to tell. Paul Revere was caught by the British and never reached Concord. Nor was he the only express rider. Many people helped spread the word that night.

DID YOU KNOW?

In 1896, Helen F. Moore wrote a poem about William Dawes in the same style as Longfellow's *Paul Revere's Ride.*

WORDS TO KNOW

stanza: a group of lines that form a part of a poem.

accurate: true, correct.

Prescott made it to Concord and alerted the town that the British were headed their way. The people of Concord rang bells and fired **volleys** of gunfire out their windows. The communication chain did not stop there. Elizabeth Rand spotted British troops and warned her neighbor, Samuel Tufts, who took off on horseback to alert others. When Solomon Bowman of Menotomy saw the British troops, he called his town's militia to arms. Dr. Martin Herrick rode out from the town of Medford and alerted the villages of Stoneham, Reading, and Lynn.

A web of patriots spread the word from town to town and house to house. When British troops marched into Lexington on the morning of April 19, the countryside of Massachusetts was ready.

Smoke of Muskets on the Lexington Green

On the morning of April 19, 1775, the sun peeked over the horizon into the small town of Lexington, Massachusetts. The meadow in town was called the Green. Villagers could graze their cattle on this land. Fifty militiamen gathered there, led by Captain John Parker.

The people of Lexington heard drums beating and **fifes** playing. The British Army had arrived, led by Lieutenant Colonel Francis Smith and Major John Pitcairn. The redcoats formed a battle line about 40 yards from the militia. Pitcairn ordered, "**Disperse**, ye rebels! Lay down your arms."

Captain Parker ordered his men to disperse, but this is where the historical accounts of the day grow muddled. As the militia began to leave the meadow, a gun went off. Even today, no one knows who fired it.

That one shot ignited a chain reaction.

Redcoats fired wildly and charged the **retreating** rebels. Major Pitcairn rode among his men. He slashed his saber, the signal to stop firing, but the soldiers kept shooting. When they ran out of ammunition, the redcoats used their **bayonets** on the colonists.

Finally, a British lieutenant found a drummer boy and ordered him to sound the cease-fire. The soldiers came to their senses. A cloud of smoke hung over the green. Officers' horses pranced anxiously. Bodies littered the ground. Eight colonists were dead and 10 wounded.

DID YOU KNOW?

About a quarter of the soldiers led by Captain John Parker were related to him.

WORDS TO KNOW

retreat: to move away from the enemy in battle.

bayonet: a sword-like blade fixed to the end of a gun for hand-to-hand fighting.

11

British Lieutenant Colonel Francis Smith ordered his men to march on to Concord. Many soldiers didn't want to march through the countryside after what had just happened. Every man in Massachusetts would want revenge. But the troops followed orders and marched down the Concord Road.

Meanwhile, as friends and neighbors tended to the dead and wounded, Captain Parker gathered his militiamen. At the end of the day, the British would have to return to Boston by the same road. Parker and his men intended to wait for them.

WORDS TO KNOW

evidence: facts or arguments that prove a case.

DID YOU KNOW?

Drums and fifes were used to communicate orders on the battlefield. Most of the musicians were boys ages 10 to 18. Nathan Futrell was only 7 when he served as a drummer boy in the Revolutionary War.

Solve History Mysteries with an Historical Toolkit

Historians use different tools and skills to figure out what happened, when it happened, and why it happened. Remember—sometimes you end an investigation with more questions than you had when you began!

Tools

- Primary sources—something made or written by a person who witnessed an event, such as letters, diaries, speeches, pottery, poems, and photographs.

- Secondary sources—something written after an event by someone who was not a witness, such as a textbook or a report based on a primary source.

Skills

- Curiosity—historical investigations start with questions.

- Analysis—historians examine different pieces of **evidence** to answer their questions.

- Interpretation—historians explain why the information matters.

Minutemen Version

On April 25, 1775, 34 **minutemen** made the following sworn statement.

[We went to the Green at about 5:00 in the morning.] "A large body of troops were marching towards us . . . the **company** began to disperse. [While] our backs were turned on the troops, we were fired on by them . . . [A] number of our men were instantly killed and wounded [.] Not a gun was fired by any [militia against the redcoats] . . . before they fired on us, [they] continued firing until we had all [escaped]."

British Soldier's Version

Lieutenant John Barker, an officer in the British Army, recorded this statement in his diary on April 19, 1775.

"At 5 o'clock we arrived there, and saw a number of people[.] I believe between 200 and 300. [They stood in green field] in the middle of town [.] We . . . continued advancing, keeping prepared against an attack . . . without intending to attack them[.] But on our coming near . . . they fired . . . two shots . . . [Then] our men . . . rushed upon them, fired and put them to flight[.] Several of them were killed, we could not tell how many."

The Shot Heard Around the World

Concord is much hillier than Lexington. The Concord militia stationed themselves a mile from town on Punkatasset Hill, where minutemen from nearby towns joined them. The colonists were led by a 60-year-old named Colonel James Barrett. When British troops reached Concord at about 8 a.m. on April 19, they **ransacked** the town while the minutemen watched from their hill. Because the colonists were outnumbered, Barrett would not let his men attack.

WORDS TO KNOW

minutemen: a special group of colonial militia who were ready to fight in a minute's notice.

company: the military name for a group of soldiers that trains and fights together.

ransack: to search for something in a way that causes damage or makes a mess.

The British hacked down the town's **liberty pole** and set it on fire. They also burned a gun carriage and some wagons. Sparks ignited the roof of the meetinghouse and it began to smolder, but the British troops put the flames out.

When the militia saw the smoke, they assumed the British were setting fire to the village.

Because of this, the militia surged toward the North Bridge, which was guarded by 115 redcoats. Both armies were nervous and frightened. As the militia began to cross the bridge, a British soldier fired. Then both sides began to shoot.

For three minutes, **musket balls** ripped through the air. Then British troops retreated and the militia stopped shooting. Several dead and wounded men from both sides lay on the ground. Because the people of Concord were armed and angry, Lieutenant Colonel Smith decided that his troops had better march back to Boston.

The British Army had a terrible time on its march back to Boston. Angry militia from 23 villages took up positions along the Concord Road. Men hid behind trees, stone fences, houses, and woodpiles. They rained musket fire down on the British. Only the arrival of **reinforcements** prevented the slaughter of Lieutenant Colonel Smith's entire force.

Finally, the British reached Bunker Hill on the edge of Boston. The British Navy was in the harbor and more British troops were stationed inside the city, so the colonial militia stopped following them.

The events of April 19, 1775, marked the beginning of America's war for independence. The British had discovered that the colonists were not just a bunch of Yankee Doodles. The militia knew the hills and valleys of the countryside and colonists were prepared to fight for their independence.

WORDS TO KNOW

reinforcements: more troops.

Yankee Doodle: slang used by the British to ridicule someone from New England.

New England: the Northeastern colonies of Massachusetts, Connecticut, New Hampshire, and Rhode Island. Today New England also includes the states of Maine and Vermont.

DID YOU KNOW?

Both colonists and British soldiers sang songs that mocked each other. When British troops marched into Lexington, they played the tune "Yankee Doodle." *Yankee* was the slang term for someone from New England. The word *doodle* meant "stupid." Colonists made up their own verses to "Yankee Doodle" that mocked the British. Today, it's considered a very American tune.

Concord Hymn

In 1837, Ralph Waldo Emerson wrote a poem called the *Concord Hymn*. This poem honored the Americans who fought in the Battle of Concord. **Read the poem here.** What do you think Emerson meant by this stanza?

Spirit, that made those heroes dare
To die, and leave their children free,
Bid Time and Nature gently spare
The shaft we raise to them and thee.

*As word of the battles at Lexington and
Concord spread, the men of Massachusetts left
their fields and workbenches. They exchanged their
plows for muskets and marched to Boston.*

By dawn on April 20, more than 16,000 soldiers from the four colonies of New England camped on the doorstep of Boston. The British Army was now trapped in the city and the colonists outnumbered the British. However, the rebel commanders did not order an attack. Colonial political leaders had not yet declared America's independence from Great Britain. Both sides waited.

Write Your Thesis Statement for Chapter 1

Now it is time to interpret what you have read in this chapter. Go to your Historical Detective Journal and find the Essential Question for this chapter.

? ESSENTIAL QUESTION

Who was responsible for the violence that occurred in Massachusetts on April 19, 1775? Would the revolution have still happened if the outcome of this first battle had been different?

Underneath this question write "Thesis Statement." Remember, a thesis statement is the main point or conclusion a historian makes after researching a specific question.

Use the knowledge you gained from the reading to write your thesis statement for Chapter 1. Share it with other students and friends. Did you all come up with the same answers? What is different about your thesis statements?

Examine Your Own Historical Sources

Supplies: *Historical Detective Journal, pen*

One of the great mysteries of the American Revolution is who fired the first shot in Lexington on the morning of April 19, 1775. The colonial militia said they did not do it. No British officer gave the order. Examine different sources and decide what you think.

1 Turn to page 2 in your journal. Label the page "Case No. 1. THE BATTLE OF LEXINGTON."

2 Below this write: "Who Fired the First Shot on the Lexington Green?"

3 Draw a vertical line to divide the page in half. Title one side "Minutemen's Version" and the other side "British Soldier's Version."

4 Read the primary sources on page 13. Record facts from each source that help answer the question. For example, how many people were present on the Green? Where were people standing? What details are different in the two accounts? Who wrote each source?

5 Now answer the question. Who fired the first shot at Lexington Green? If you still have questions, what kinds of sources would help you uncover the truth?

ACTIVITY

Signal Lantern

Supplies: *medium-size empty tin can with label removed, scissors, 1 piece of white paper, water, freezer, towel, tape, large nail, hammer, 12-inch-long piece of thin wire (30 centimeters), tea candle and matches, dry spaghetti*

Robert Newman was the caretaker of the Old North Church. On the night of April 18, 1775, he climbed the tall steeple in total darkness. When he reached the top, he lit two lanterns and held them to the window. This signaled to the patriots on the other side of the river that British troops had taken the water route to Concord. Ask an adult to help you make your own signal lantern.

1 Cut a piece of paper large enough to fit around the outside of the can.

2 Fill the can with water and freeze until solid.

3 While the water is freezing, draw a simple design of dots, diamonds, or squares on the paper.

4 Lay the can of frozen water on a towel on a flat surface. Tape your paper design to the outside of the can.

5 Use the nail and hammer to puncture a hole in the can about every half inch along the design on your paper.

6 Pound two holes on opposite sides along the top of the can.

7 Remove the paper from the outside of the can. Soak the can in hot water until the ice melts. Let the can air dry.

8 Slide the wire through the holes at the top of the can to make a handle. Bend the ends up so the wire does not slip out and poke you.

9 Place a tea candle in the bottom of the can. Ask an adult to use a piece of dry spaghetti to light the candle. Now you are ready to alert the land!

DID YOU KNOW?

Robert Newman and John Pulling were the rebels who risked capture to hang to lanterns in the Old North Church on April 18, 1775.

One If By Land, and Two If By Sea

The phrase "One if by land, and two if by sea" was written by Henry Wadsworth Longfellow in his famous poem of Paul Revere's ride. It refers to the lanterns hung in the tower of the Old North Church in Boston, which signaled to the patriots that the British were coming over the water instead of marching over land. Every year on April 18, two lanterns are hung in the tower of the Old North Church to commemorate the bravery of the patriots.

Chapter 2

The Roots of Rebellion

The Revolutionary War began on April 19, 1775. What caused the Americans to revolt against their mother country? This is a complicated question with no simple answer. To understand, we must go back to the beginning of the story.

What caused the colonists to resist British policies before and after the French and Indian War? Were the colonists right or wrong?

Who Stole the Cookie From the Cookie Jar?

Imagine an open cookie jar on the counter in the kitchen. The cookies are huge and chock-full of chocolate chips. The aroma of butter and brown sugar makes your stomach growl. A sign says: "Cookies, $1 each." No one is there to collect the money, so you leave empty-handed, belly still growling.

The next day, the jar is there again, but this time it holds peanut butter cookies sprinkled with sugar. The price is still one dollar. Once again, no one is there. This time, you take a cookie and gobble it up. It's delicious!

Since nobody is there to collect your money, you decide it's okay to just take a cookie.

You help yourself the next day, and the next, and get used to taking the cookie without paying for it. You forget that it is supposed to cost one dollar.

Then one day, when you slip your hand in the jar, a trap closes around it. You can't escape! A police officer arrives and hauls you off to jail for stealing. Do you think this is fair or unfair?

WORDS TO KNOW

smuggle: to move goods illegally in or out of a country.

import: to bring a product into a country to be sold.

merchant: a person who buys and sells goods for a **profit.**

profit: the money made by selling an item or service for more than it cost.

enforce: to carry out a law.

Christopher Columbus: an Italian explorer who landed in the Americas while seeking a route to China.

In 1763, the American colonists were caught with their hands in the cookie jar. Instead of stealing cookies, they were **smuggling** goods. British law required the colonists to pay taxes on goods **imported** into America. But colonial **merchants** were purchasing sugar and molasses from the Caribbean Islands and sneaking the goods into America to avoid paying the tax. Great Britain ignored this smuggling for a long time, then suddenly began to **enforce** the law. The colonists were caught by surprise and they were not happy.

A New World for a New Life

By 1763, the American colonies were already 156 years old. Europeans had begun to colonize North America shortly after **Christopher Columbus** landed in the Caribbean in 1492. While the Spanish conquered much of Central America and the area that would become Florida, the land between the Appalachian Mountains and the Rocky Mountains was claimed by the French. The British settled along the Atlantic coastline.

The first British settlers colonized Jamestown, Virginia, in 1607. These early adventurers sought gold in America. Three-quarters of the settlers died during the first winter, but more British colonists came. Eventually, this region became known as the Southern Colonies and included Maryland, Virginia, North Carolina, South Carolina, and Georgia.

Trials and Tribulations

(PS)

This quote from a letter of a Jamestown settler gives a description of some of the trouble early colonists faced. What qualities does the writer display that might have helped him **endure** his hardships? What can we learn about his life in Jamestown?

"My comendations remembred, I hartely [wish] your welfare for god be thanked I am now in good health, but my brother and my wyfe are dead aboute a yeare pass'd And touchinge the busynesse that I came hither is nothing yett performed, by reason of my sicknesse & weaknesse I was not able to travell up and downe the hills and dales of these countries but doo nowe intend every daye to walke up and downe the hills for good Mineralls here is both golde silver and copper to be had . . . ."

The **economy** of the southern region was based on tobacco and other **crops** such as **indigo** and rice. Slaves worked huge tracts of land on farms called **plantations**.

The British colonists tried to force Native Americans into slavery, but they rebelled or died from European diseases.

Immigrants from Great Britain also settled in New England. The economy of this region, which included the colonies of Massachusetts, Connecticut, Rhode Island, and New Hampshire, was based on small family farms. In the cities along the coast, many dockworkers, rope-makers, and merchants made their living from the shipping industry. There were few slaves in New England.

WORDS TO KNOW

endure: to experience for a long time.

economy: the wealth and resources of an area or country.

crop: a plant grown for food and other uses.

indigo: a plant used to make dark blue dyes.

plantation: a large farm in a hot climate. In colonial times, plantations used slaves as workers.

immigrant: a person who leaves his or her own country to live in another country.

Between New England and the Southern Colonies lay the Middle Colonies of New York, New Jersey, Pennsylvania, and Delaware. Corn and wheat grew in the rich soil of this area. As in New England, people lived on small family farms. The Middle Colonies also had two important colonial cities. Philadelphia was the center of colonial American culture and New York City had a bustling harbor.

The first European settlers in what is now New York were Dutch. In 1626, they bought the island of Manhattan from the native people for tools, farming equipment, cloth, and beads.

During the 1600s, most of the immigrants to the 13 colonies came from Great Britain, but during the 1700s that changed.

By the 1760s, only two-thirds of the white colonists were British.

Many Germans had settled in Pennsylvania, and the Scots and Irish made homes in the Appalachian Mountains of the Southern and Middle colonies.

Slave traders brought African people to the American colonies by force. The first shipment of slaves landed in Jamestown in 1619. By 1750, more than 1 million Africans had been kidnapped from their homeland. They were **shackled** like cattle in slave ships and transported to the **New World**. While only 25 percent of colonists owned slaves and most were used in the Southern Colonies, the economies of all three regions depended on the slave trade.

WORDS TO KNOW

shackle: to chain a prisoner's wrists or ankles together.

New World: what is now America. It was called the New World by people from Europe because it was new to them.

DID YOU KNOW? ★★★★★★

In colonial times, when a woman married, her husband became owner of all her wealth. When George Washington married Martha Custis, he gained 300 slaves and 17,000 acres of land.

A Slave's Point of View

Olaudah Equiano was only 11 years old when he was kidnapped from his home in North Africa and sold into slavery. He eventually bought his own freedom, joined the British Navy, and wrote an autobiography about his life as a slave. Here is his description of his own capture:

"One day, when all our people were gone out to their works as usual, and only I and my dear sister were left to mind the house, two men and a woman got over our walls, and in a moment seized us both, and, without giving us time to cry out, or make resistance, they stopped our mouths, and ran off with us into the nearest wood."

Do you think Olaudah's book helped change the way the public felt about slavery? Why? **You can read more of *The Interesting Narrative of the Life of Olaudah Equiano*.**

Democracy Develops in America

The American colonies were technically governed by Great Britain. However, the colonies were 3,000 miles away from London, which was the capital of Great Britain and the British **Empire**. As this was long before the invention of the airplane and the dangerous journey from Britain to North America took at least a month by ship, visits and communication between Great Britain and the colonies were rare. The colonies were generally left to develop their own governments. These were modeled after the British system.

Britain was ruled by a **limited monarchy**. This meant that the power of King George was controlled by a group of lawmakers called **Parliament**. British citizens were guaranteed certain **rights** and liberties. These included the right to a **jury trial** and the right to have someone represent you in government if you were going to be taxed by that government.

When British colonists settled in the American colonies, they brought their beliefs about liberty with them.

The colonists in Virginia created a **legislative assembly** in 1619 called the House of Burgesses. These representatives made laws for the colony of Virginia. Although only white, property-owning males were allowed to vote, the House of Burgesses was the first official example of American **democracy**. Soon, all 13 colonies had their own legislative assemblies.

During the next 150 years, the colonies grew used to governing themselves. Can you blame the colonists for being unhappy when Great Britain decided to change the rules?

WORDS TO KNOW

legislative assembly: the group within the government that makes laws.

democracy: a system of government where the people choose who will represent and govern them.

DID YOU KNOW?

By the 1760s, Great Britain also had colonies in Canada and the Caribbean, and trading posts in Indonesia, India, and the west coast of Africa. Britain was a huge empire. An old saying goes, "The sun never sets on the British Empire." What do you think this saying means?

The American Economy

Most parents want the best for their children—to grow up healthy, get a good education, and become successful adults. As the mother country of the 13 colonies, Great Britain wanted something a little different for her children.

27

WORDS TO KNOW

In the 1600s and 1700s, people believed in **mercantilism**. This is the idea that a nation should **export** more products than it imports while collecting as much gold and silver as possible. Great Britain established colonies to get rich. It wanted to import valuable American goods, such as tobacco, and have the colonists buy goods grown in other British colonies, such as tea and sugar.

As the 13 colonies developed, they began to trade with Spain, France, and Holland. Great Britain feared losing control of American trade and passed a series of laws to prevent this, such as the Molasses Act of 1733. American colonists had been buying molasses from the French Caribbean Islands because it was cheaper than molasses from the British Caribbean Islands. Parliament declared that all French molasses bought by colonists would be taxed, making French molasses more expensive than British molasses.

The Triangle Trade

The "triangle trade" of slavery lasted 250 years. Europeans traveled on ships to West Africa to trade copper, cloth, guns, and beads for slaves. These slaves were shipped to South America or the Caribbean to labor in sugarcane fields. This sugar was made into molasses and sent to New England to make rum. The rum was shipped back to England and eventually used to purchase more African slaves. These slaves were sent to the Caribbean to grow more sugar or to the Southern Colonies to work on tobacco plantations. Each leg of the triangle held up the other two.

New England merchants, including John Hancock, resented Parliament for wanting to cut into their profits.

WORDS TO KNOW

customs agent: a government official who collects taxes on imports and exports.

Great Britain did not have enough money to enforce the law. For years, Hancock and other merchants smuggled molasses into Massachusetts and never paid taxes on it.

Here's how smuggling worked: A colonial ship captain would stop on a deserted stretch of beach and unload most of the molasses. Then he sailed into Boston, where a royal **customs agent** inspected the ship and taxed the captain for the small amount of molasses still on the ship. Later, the captain collected the rest of the molasses from the beach—and the inspectors never saw it!

Everyone knew what was going on, but no one in North America cared. Smuggling became a respectable trade and people such as Hancock grew rich. This lack of enforcement of the law was known as "salutary neglect." This meant that the colonies developed their own effective systems of trade and government while Great Britain left them alone.

WORDS TO KNOW

fertile: good for growing crops.

treaty: a written agreement between two countries.

allied: joined together.

tyrant: a cruel ruler who denies people their rights.

The French and Indian War

North America was a prize that both France and Great Britain wanted. In 1756, they went to war over the **fertile** land of the Ohio River Valley. Most Native American tribes sided with the French because they trusted the French more than the British not to take all the land. Colonial troops fought on the side of the British.

The French lost the war. A **treaty** signed in 1763 officially ended France's power over lands east of the Mississippi River. The bloodshed did not stop with this agreement, however. Many of the Native Americans who had **allied** with the French refused to accept the surrender terms. The Ottawa Chief Pontiac united several tribes together and they attacked British forts around the Great Lakes. The Native Americans succeeded in capturing several forts, but, ultimately, British reinforcements proved too strong. In 1766, the rebelling Native American nations and the British negotiated peace.

DID YOU KNOW? In 1754, when Britain and France were still at peace before the French and Indian War, a young major in the British Army named George Washington led an attack on a French fort. This attack began the French and Indian War. It was the aftermath of this war that led to the American Revolution.

The colonists celebrated the end of the French and Indian War. They expected that all that rich land in the Ohio River Valley would be theirs. Soon, though, their hopes were shattered.

On October 25, 1760, King George II had died at age 77. His 22-year-old son, George III, took the throne. British subjects everywhere loved their kings, but it would not be long before many American colonists began to call King George III a **tyrant**.

Native American Good Sense

(PS)

Relations between the Native Americans and colonists were difficult from the earliest settlements. In 1609, Powhatan, leader of the Powhatan tribes in what would become Virginia, gave a speech in which he pleaded with white men to take away their guns and swords. How might history have been different if the British and French did as Powhatan asked?

"Why will you take by force what you may obtain by love? Why will you destroy us who supply you with food? What can you get by war? . . . We are unarmed, and willing to give you what you ask, if you come in a friendly manner . . . .

"I am not so simple as not to know it is better to eat good meat, sleep comfortably, live quietly with my women and children, laugh and be merry with the English, and being their friend, trade for their copper and hatchets, than to run away from them . . . .

"Take away your guns and swords, the cause of all our jealousy, or you may die in the same manner."

When King George III learned in 1763 that Pontiac was leading a rebellion in the Great Lakes region, he quickly issued a **proclamation**. An invisible line would separate the American colonies from the Native American lands west of the Appalachian Mountains. Colonists were forbidden to cross this boundary and enter the Ohio River Valley.

WORDS TO KNOW

proclamation: a public announcement.

The British government hoped that the Proclamation Act of 1763 would calm the Native Americans, who feared that white farmers were planning to take their lands.

The British Army set up forts along the Proclamation Line to enforce the law. Since the forts were designed to protect colonists against Native American attacks, Parliament believed the colonists should pay to build and maintain them. The colonists disagreed. The prize they had fought for—the Ohio River Valley—had been snatched from their hands.

There was more trouble brewing. The French and Indian War had doubled Britain's national **debt**. King George and Parliament knew they needed to bring in more money. One way to do this was by raising taxes. A new prime minister, George Grenville, was elected to Parliament in 1763. He proposed a solution: raise taxes on American colonists.

DID YOU KNOW?

At the end of the French and Indian War, the colonists paid an average of $1.20 a year in taxes. The typical person living in England paid $30 a year in taxes. When American colonists began to rebel against taxes, many citizens in England could not understand what they were so upset about.

? THESIS STATEMENT

Now it's time to interpret what you have read in this chapter and answer the Essential Question:

What caused the colonists to resist British policies before and after the French and Indian War? Were the colonists right or wrong?

Make Your Own Wintertime Molasses Candy

Supplies: *2 cake pans (9 by 13 inches), fresh snow, 1 cup molasses, ½ cup brown sugar, saucepan, stove, wooden spoon, candy thermometer, ceramic pitcher, plate, Ziploc bag (see chart in glossary for metric equivalents)*

After sugarcane is boiled down into sugar crystals, the leftover liquid is called molasses. You can make up a batch of this molasses candy and see why colonial Americans loved molasses! CAUTION: Boiling molasses and brown sugar is HOT! Get an adult to help you!

1 Fill the two cake pans with fresh snow and keep them outside.

2 Heat molasses and brown sugar in the saucepan over medium heat, stirring often.

3 Boil the mixture until it reaches 245 degrees. Have an adult pour it into the pitcher.

4 Drizzle the molasses mixture on the snow. When the candy is cool and hard, it's ready to eat! Store leftovers in a Ziploc bag in the freezer.

ACTIVITY

Build Your Own Population Graph

Supplies: *graph paper, pencil*

In the 1750s, Benjamin Franklin wrote a series of essays about America's rapid population growth. He predicted that by the middle of the 1800s, more people would live in America than in England—and he was right! Use the data chart on the next page to make a line graph that demonstrates the rapid population growth in the 13 colonies.

1 On your graph paper, a few rows up from the bottom, draw an X axis from left to right. Label this "Millions of People." How many people should each square represent? You need to mark off even amounts starting at zero and going up to 3,000,000.

2 Draw a Y axis up the left side, a few columns from the left edge, starting at the left point of the X axis. Label this "Years." How many squares should each decade represent? Mark off the Y axis with the years provided in the chart, starting with 1700.

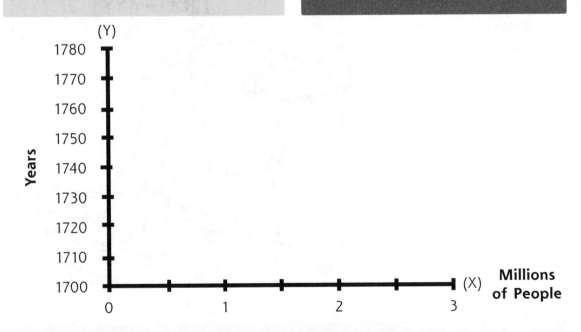

3 Plot the population data for each year. Use a dot to mark each data point. For example, in 1700 there were just more than 250,000 people in the colonies, so you find the year 1700 on the Y axis and move right across the X axis to the number of people equaling just more than 250,000 people. Place your point there, as in the sample graph below.

4 When you've plotted all the years and populations from the chart at the right on your graph, connect the dots to form a line graph.

Population Growth of the 13 Colonies	
Years	**Total Population**
1700	250,888
1710	331,7111
1720	466,185
1730	629,445
1740	905,563
1750	1,170,760
1760	1,593,625
1770	2,148,076
1780	2,780,369

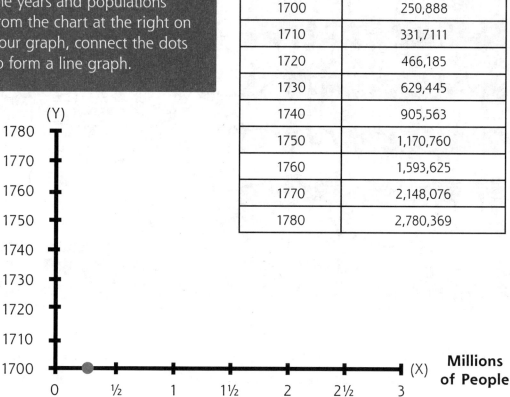

TRY THIS: Can you calculate . . .

* How many more people lived in the American colonies in 1760 than lived there in 1720?

* If the population in 1800 was five times greater than it was in 1750, what was the population in 1800?

Chapter 3
A Harbor Full of Tea

On August 26, 1765, an angry mob gathered outside the house of Massachusetts Lieutenant Governor Thomas Hutchinson while he and his family were eating dinner. When the mob began to hack at the front door with axes, Hutchinson and his family fled. Minutes later, the gang burst in. They chopped up the furniture and stripped paintings off the walls. They destroyed the governor's formal gardens and drained his wine cellar.

How did the views of patriots and loyalists differ in the years leading up to the war? Would you have been a revolutionary in colonial America?

The mob targeted Hutchinson because he was a powerful man who supported the new laws that Parliament had made for the colonies. These laws enraged many colonists. The topic that most angered the mob was something that Americans today usually take for granted—taxes.

The Stamp Act

The British Parliament announced the Stamp Act in March 1765. With this new law, documents such as newspapers, prayer books, playing cards, and diplomas had to be printed on stamped paper that had been taxed. If a document did not have a stamp, it was not legal. The tax only amounted to a small amount of money, but it was the first time that Parliament had directly taxed colonists, and they were furious.

For some colonists, the tax itself was not the issue.
They were already angry for other reasons.

poverty: the state of being very poor.

principle: an important idea or belief that guides an individual or community.

slogan: a phrase used by a business or other group to get attention.

rallying: causing a group of people to have new energy and enthusiasm for something.

Since the end of the French and Indian War, the people of New England had struggled with **poverty**. Many people were homeless and out of work. These "strolling poor" wandered from town to town looking for jobs. They were hungry, angry, and looking for someone to blame.

Other colonists were upset about the **principle** behind the Stamp Act. Merchants, lawyers, and other wealthy colonists thought it was unfair to be taxed when they could not vote for members of Parliament.

In 1765, Patrick Henry, a new representative in the Virginia House of Burgesses, introduced a series of statements called the Virginia Resolves. These argued that the colonists should have the same liberties as people who lived in Great Britain. One of these liberties was that taxes could only be raised by representatives elected by the people. This liberty became a **slogan**: "No taxation without representation." It became the **rallying** cry of the revolution.

Resistance

Assemblies in almost every colony quickly adopted the Virginia Resolves. In October, seven colonies sent representatives to a meeting called the Stamp Act Congress. This meeting was the first time leaders of the colonies united.

They issued a statement: Parliament had no authority to tax American colonists.

On the day the Stamp Act was to take effect, the colonists flew flags at half mast and church bells tolled in mourning. No colonial governor enforced the law. People refused to buy stamped paper. Newspapers shut down their presses rather than print on stamped paper. Many businesses simply ignored the law. Documents were bought and sold on unstamped paper.

WORDS TO KNOW

boycott: refusing to buy or use a product.

civil disobedience: refusing to obey certain laws or pay taxes as a peaceful form of political protest.

nonviolent: characterized by not using physical force or power.

effigy: a fake model of a person.

The colonial **boycott** was born. These colonists were practicing **civil disobedience** by using **nonviolent** methods to protest what they thought was an unjust law.

However, not all colonists were nonviolent. A secret rebel group called the Sons of Liberty encouraged mobs to march through the streets of most major cities. From the North to the South, protesters burned **effigies** of stamp distributors and destroyed their property.

Stop the Presses!

The *Pennsylvania Journal* stopped publishing when the Stamp Act was passed. **Read the story published in the *Pennsylvania Journal* the day after the Stamp Act was enforced.** How does the writer express his opinions about the Stamp Act? What words show how he feels?

The Stamp Act was a turning point for many colonists. For the first time, they realized that they were second-class citizens of the British Empire. A colonist could never be elected to Parliament or serve as prime minister or be a top commander in the British Army.

DID YOU KNOW?

The Sons of Liberty were semi-secret societies that sprang up in every colony. They resisted British laws, often using violence. Some people today would call the Sons of Liberty terrorists.

John Adams was only 30 years old in 1765, but he recognized the significance of the events of that year. He said the Stamp Act was "an enormous engine . . . battering down all the rights and liberties of America." No one was talking about it yet, but the seeds of American independence had been planted.

Parliament debated how to handle the rebellious colonists. Some members wanted to use force to put the rebels in their place. Others cautioned patience.

All members of Parliament agreed on one thing—they wanted to prove who was boss.

Parliament **repealed** the Stamp Act and Americans throughout the colonies celebrated. Church bells rang. Thanksgiving sermons were preached from every church. Days of celebration occurred in cities, towns, and villages.

WORDS TO KNOW

repeal: to withdraw.

Busy with all their celebrations, the colonists neglected to pay attention to the Declaratory Act. On the same day that the Stamp Act was repealed, Parliament issued a law that boldly stated that Parliament had the power to make laws for America "in all cases whatsoever." Parliament was sending that strong reminder to the colonies that Britain was in charge.

Townshend Acts

After the repeal of the Stamp Act, Parliament came up with a new idea for raising money. The Townshend Acts were a series of laws that taxed tea, paper, lead, glass, and paint. The colonists howled in protest!

But patriot leaders were cautious. They wanted all 13 colonies to unite against the British laws. They feared that **conservative** colonists might be irritated by **rioting** mobs such as those that protested the Stamp Act. Huge crowds gathered around liberty poles in all major cities to protest the Townshend Acts, but the Sons of Liberty kept a lid on the violence.

Matters worsened when two British **regiments** were sent to Boston to enforce the anti-smuggling laws. The Quartering Act required that colonists pay to feed and shelter redcoats stationed in their towns. Bostonians saw these troops as a clear sign of the **tyranny** of Great Britain. The city was ready to explode.

WORDS TO KNOW

conservative: someone who is cautious about change.

riot: a gathering of people protesting something, which gets out of control and violent.

regiment: a unit of soldiers.

tyranny: cruel and unfair treatment by people in power.

Give Me Liberty or Give Me . . . . What Did You Say?

For the past 200 years, textbooks across the country have credited Patrick Henry with uttering this stirring phrase on the eve of the revolution: "Almighty God! I know not what course others may take; but as for me, give me liberty or give me death."

Henry never actually said this. In 1805, an attorney named William Wirt decided to write about Patrick Henry's life. The problem for Wirt was that Henry never wrote any of his speeches down. He made them up as he spoke. So, Wirt had to imagine what Henry might have said. Would Patrick Henry really have given up his life for liberty? We will probably never know. What does this quote tell you about historical research? Why is it important to be accurate when you write about history?

A Massacre or a Mob?

At 9:15 p.m. on March 5, 1770, the alarm bell rang in Boston. People grabbed their leather fire brigade buckets and raced toward the sound. In an age when almost every building was made of wood, a fire could destroy the city in minutes. Soon, 200 men and boys had gathered on King Street in front of the Customs House. But there was no fire.

Instead, colonists found a squad of eight British soldiers led by Captain Thomas Preston standing guard. The crowd began to harass the soldiers. They cursed, jeered, and threw snowballs and chunks of ice at the men.

One man in the crowd yelled, "Come on you rascals, you bloody-backs, you lobster scoundrels. Fire if you dare."

No one knows for certain what happened next. We only know that a shot rang out. Then someone in the crowd clubbed one of the soldiers and struck Captain Preston. The troops jabbed the attacker with their bayonets. Another soldier raised his gun.

The soldier fired, and other soldiers quickly fired their muskets, too. As they reloaded their weapons, Captain Preston bellowed, "Do not fire!"

DID YOU KNOW?

Soon people from New Hampshire to Georgia had heard about the Boston Massacre and believed that the British had launched an attack on innocent Bostonians.

When the wind blew the musket smoke away, the crowd saw the horror that lay before them. Eleven men had been shot. Three died instantly, another died a few hours later, and a fifth man died the next day. The remaining wounded survived. Throughout the night, people called, "To arms! To arms!" Drums banged and church bells tolled, but there was no more violence.

In the following days, the Boston Town Council sent Samuel Adams to speak with the commander of British troops in the city. Adams insisted that both regiments be removed from the city or "the rage of the people would vent itself." The troops were relocated to an island in Boston Harbor.

propaganda: the use of information, often false or exaggerated, to persuade people.

massacre: the deliberate killing of many people.

WORDS TO KNOW

The Sons of Liberty seized on the events of March 5, 1770, for **propaganda** purposes. Paul Revere copied an artist's sketch of the scene, made an engraving of it, and then made colored prints from this engraving. Advertisements for Revere's prints were published in newspapers across the colonies. He used the phrase, "The Horrid **Massacre**," to describe the event.

PS

Paul Revere's *Boston Massacre*

Examine prints made by Paul Revere. Why did colonists react strongly to it? Have you ever seen illustrations in newspapers or magazines that make you feel a certain way? Why do artists draw things that might exaggerate the truth?

A Tea Party

The Townshend Acts could not be enforced. London merchants were upset because colonial boycotts had caused their profits to plummet. Three days before the Boston Massacre, Parliament repealed all of the Townshend Acts, except the one on tea, a drink the colonists loved and bought plenty of. Parliament did not realize that this innocent drink would bring the British one step closer to war.

Today many Americans begin their day with a cup of coffee. In the 1700s colonists preferred tea. The East India Tea Company was an important British company, but it was not managed properly. By the early 1770s, the company was almost broke.

In order to help the company, the British government gave it a **monopoly**. This meant that the East India Tea Company was the only company allowed to import tea into America. The company lowered the price of its tea, but Parliament tacked on a tea tax. British ships loaded with tea headed for New York, Charleston, Philadelphia, and Boston.

Colonists were upset that they could not purchase tea from other countries, and they were angry about the tax on tea.

Leaders organized a massive tea boycott. People from New England to Georgia brewed raspberry tea or sassafras tea or started drinking coffee. Their beloved tea was not worth taxation without representation.

The Adams Family—Cousins Samuel and John

Samuel Adams is often called the mastermind of the American Revolution. People said he stirred crowds to violence. This rumor was actually spread by his enemies, who hoped the British would arrest him. Adams was a skilled writer and a good organizer, but he disapproved of violence by Boston mobs.

John Adams, Samuel's cousin, was a lawyer. He defended the British soldiers charged with massacring colonists in Boston on March 5, 1770. He was a patriot, but he knew that what happened in Boston was a tragedy, not a massacre. "Facts are stubborn things," Adams told the jury, "and whatever may be our wishes . . . they cannot alter the evidence." The jury was convinced. Most of the soldiers were found not guilty.

On November 28, 1773, the *Dartmouth* sailed into Boston Harbor with 114 chests of tea on board. Massachusetts law said that once the tea was unloaded, the owner had to pay the tea tax within 20 days or the government could seize the cargo. Massachusetts Governor Thomas Hutchinson was determined that the tea would be unloaded and the tax paid.

DID YOU KNOW?

In today's money, the value of the tea dumped in the Boston Harbor is $700,000.

Bostonians demanded that the East India Tea Company return the tea to England. Days passed and the standoff continued. Then two more ships arrived in the harbor loaded with more East India Tea Company tea!

The night before the tea tax deadline, a cold rain fell on 5,000 people gathered at the Old South Meeting House. The crowd watched as approximately 100 young men dressed as **Mohawk** warriors boarded the three ships, chopped open all 342 crates, and dumped the tea into the harbor. The crowd watched in silence—no ships were damaged and no one was injured. John Adams wrote in his diary, "This is the most magnificent movement of all. There is a dignity . . . in this last effort of the Patriots that I greatly admire."

WORDS TO KNOW

Mohawk: a tribe of Native Americans, part of the Iroquois Confederacy.

George Hewes of the Boston Tea Party (PS)

George Hewes was one of the men who boarded the *Dartmouth* to dump the tea overboard. He offers this first-hand account of the morning after the event.

"The next morning, after we had cleared the ships of the tea, it was discovered that very considerable quantities of it were floating upon the surface of the water; and to prevent the possibility of any of its being saved for use, a number of small boats were manned by sailors and citizens, who rowed them into those parts of the harbor wherever the tea was visible, and by beating it with oars and paddles so thoroughly drenched it as to render its entire destruction inevitable."

Why did the sailors and citizens want to destroy the tea completely? What did this show about their level of emotion?

The Coercive Acts

Outrage swept across England with the news of the Boston Tea Party. Newspaper articles blamed Samuel Adams and John Hancock. The British public demanded these men be arrested for **treason**.

Members of Parliament were as angry as the public. In March 1774, to punish Massachusetts for the Boston Tea Party, they passed the Coercive Acts, closing Boston Harbor until the tea was paid for. The Massachusetts Assembly was put under British control. Town meetings, a tradition of local government in New England, were banned. If a colonist was charged with a crime, his trial could be held in England instead of in his own community, but British officials could not be charged with a crime in Massachusetts. Parliament knew these tough rules could start a war.

> **WORDS TO KNOW**
> **treason:** actions that go against one's own country.

British officials believed that the colonies were divided and were a "poor species of fighting men." They were certain that a few battles would bring the colonists into line.

47

When Boston leaders heard of the Coercive Acts, the Boston Committee of Correspondence acted immediately. These committees maintained communication between colonies. The Boston committee sent riders, including Paul Revere, from city to city to ask for supplies while the harbor was closed. The committee also asked for other colonies to stand up to the British to stop the spread of unfair treatment.

Aid poured in from as far south as Georgia, and the colonies began to unite.

The First Continental Congress

In the fall of 1774, representatives from all colonies except Georgia gathered in Carpenter's Hall in Philadelphia, Pennsylvania, to form the **First Continental Congress**. The **delegates** were divided about how to respond to the Coercive Acts and the meetings went on for days. John Adams described them as "nibbling and quibbling." Delegates from Boston wanted swift action to let Britain know that the Coercive Acts had to go. The Middle Colonies had grown rich off British trade and feared losing their wealth. They wanted to smooth things over.

The First Continental Congress came to a **compromise**. They declared that all colonists had the basic rights of life, liberty, and property. They also agreed to enforce a complete boycott of all British imports until the Coercive Acts were repealed. The Congress recommended that each colony should begin training a militia.

WORDS TO KNOW

First Congressional Congress: delegates from each colony except Georgia who met to discuss the colonies' reaction to Britain.

delegate: someone sent to a meeting to represent others.

compromise: an agreement made when each side gives in a little.

King George III quickly made his opinion clear. On November 18, 1774, he wrote a letter to his prime minister. It said, "The New England governments are in a state of rebellion, blows must decide if they are subject to this country or independent."

A Divided People

As 1774 came to an end, colonists debated their future. On one side were the patriots, also called the Whigs. They wanted to separate from Great Britain and form an independent nation. On the opposite side were the loyalists, or the Tories. They wanted to repair their relationship with Great Britain and remain a colony. Many colonists did not fit neatly into either category.

Do you think that Americans today are easily divided into two political parties, such as Democrats and Republicans? Or do many people agree with certain beliefs from both parties?

Most loyalists were wealthy landowners and businessmen with close ties to British merchants. They believed that the strength of American business depended upon trade with Great Britain. Patriots insisted that the British had restricted colonial trade to benefit themselves. If the colonies were free to trade with anyone, the economy would grow stronger.

Colonists were separated by differing values as well. Loyalists loved King George. Being citizens of the British Empire was part of their identities. They believed that to even think about independence was treason. In contrast, patriots defined themselves as American, not British.

WORDS TO KNOW

value: a strongly held belief about what is valuable, important, or acceptable.

49

Whigs and Tories

Originally, the word *tory* meant outlaw and *whig* meant country **bumpkin**. By the 1680s, the Whigs and Tories were two political parties that disagreed about who had the rightful claim to be the British king. In the 1770s, Tories represented people who believed the king should have lots of power, while Whigs felt the people should have a stronger say in the government.

Both loyalists and patriots worried about their security, but in different ways. Loyalists feared that without a king and Parliament, uneducated, angry mobs would rule the streets. Patriots thought the British government was the real danger, and without Britain's unfair laws, there would no reason to protest.

DID YOU KNOW?

Slaves in Massachusetts wrote **petitions** to the colonial government. They said freedom was a natural right of all people, including slaves. Massachusetts ended slavery in 1780.

The tensions that seethed between the Whigs and the Tories and between colonists and the British people set the stage for the bloody battles of Lexington and Concord in April 1775 that you read about in Chapter 1.

WORDS TO KNOW

bumpkin: an awkward, simple person; today we would say hick or redneck.

petition: a formal, written request.

? THESIS STATEMENT

Now it's time to interpret what you have read in this chapter and answer the Essential Question:

How did the views of patriots and loyalists differ in the years leading up to the war? Would you have been a revolutionary in colonial America?

Investigate Your Own Taxes, Taxes Everywhere

Supplies: *an old receipt, pencil, paper*

Taxes are as much a part of life today as they were in colonial days. But there's big difference—we no longer have taxation without representation! What are taxes like in your lifetime? How are they different than they were before the revolution?

1 You have to do some math to understand the impact of taxes. Imagine that you want to buy a shirt priced at $25.00. The cashier rings up your purchase and the total bill comes to $26.25. Use these formulas to calculate the percentage of tax that was paid on the shirt:

$$\$26.25 - \$25.00 = 1.25$$

(total cost − price of the shirt = amount of the tax)

$$1.25 \div 25.00 = .05 \text{ (or 5\%)}$$

(amount of the tax ÷ price of the shirt = percentage of the tax)

2 Look at all the numbers listed on your receipt. Circle the taxes that were collected when the item or items were purchased. Calculate what percent tax you paid using the formulas above.

TRY THIS: Collect receipts from a day's worth of purchases. How much money do you pay in taxes on an average day? Why are some items taxed and others are not? What does the government use the tax money for? What can you do to tell government leaders what you think about taxes?

ACTIVITY

Investigate Your Own Historical Accuracy

Supplies: *picture of the* Boston Massacre *by Paul Revere (QR code on page 44), white paper, colored pencils*

Paul Revere's engraving of what happened in Boston on March 5, 1770, is one of the most important pieces of propaganda in American history. Many of the "facts" in Revere's engraving were not historically accurate. Use the summary of the event that you read in this chapter to correct his historical errors.

1 Make a sketch of the Boston Massacre based on the account you read. Consider the following elements.

* What time did the event occur?

* What was the weather like?

* How many soldiers were present? How many citizens?

* How was the crowd behaving before shots were fired? How were the soldiers behaving?

* What was the sequence of events?

2 Study your drawing. Who does your drawing blame for the events of March 5, 1770? Compare your drawing to Revere's print. How are they different?

TRY THIS: Why did Paul Revere draw the sketch to portray the British as the bad guys? Do you think history would have happened differently if he'd stuck to the truth? Can you think of other times when propaganda influenced the outcome of history?

Design Your Own Political Bumper Sticker

Supplies: *paper, colored pencils, 3-inch by 8-inch piece of poster board (8 centimeters by 20 centimeters)*

If you lived in 1775, would you have been a patriot or a loyalist? Why? Bumper stickers are a form of propaganda and a chance to tell the world your views!

1 Create a short, punchy, persuasive slogan. Can you think of political bumper stickers you see today? Look these examples of political slogans from American presidential candidates. Can you be more creative?

★ John Fremont (1856) *Free Soil, Free Labor, Free Speech, Free Men, Frémont.*

★ Herbert Hoover (1928) *A chicken in every pot and a car in every garage.*

★ Franklin D. Roosevelt (1932) *Happy days are here again.*

★ Bill Clinton (1992) *It's the economy, stupid.*

2 Write your slogan on the poster board to make your bumper sticker. Decorate it so that's it's both eye-catching and easy to read.

TRY THIS: Create a new bumper sticker for the political party you don't believe in. Is this harder or easier to write?

Chapter 4
A Declaration Is Made

Forty thousand people lived in Philadelphia in 1775. Carts and wagons rattled down paved streets. At night people strolled down brick sidewalks illuminated by street lights. Tall elms and poplar trees shaded brick homes and government buildings. Cows grazed on the **commons**.

? ESSENTIAL QUESTION

What caused American leaders to finally declare independence in July 1776? How would our country today be different without the Declaration of Independence?

WORDS TO KNOW

Second Continental Congress: delegates from the colonies who met in 1775 to discuss whether or not America should declare its independence.

The State House was a red brick building at the intersection of Chestnut and Walnut streets. Crowned by a 68-foot-tall bell tower, it was a skyscraper by eighteenth-century standards. On May 10, 1775, 56 delegates from all 13 colonies gathered there in Philadelphia for the first meeting of the **Second Continental Congress**.

With the Lexington and Concord slaughter fresh in every delegate's mind, the Congress voted to supply the Massachusetts militia with gunpowder and flour. They also decided to form a new Continental Army, commanded by George Washington.

The bloodshed in Massachusetts was only the beginning.

Battle of Bunker Hill

On the night of June 16, 1775, hundreds of colonial militiamen marched toward Boston. Their goal was to build defenses on Bunker Hill in Charlestown. In the dark, the soldiers completely missed Bunker Hill and set up on Breed's Hill instead. This high ground overlooked the British Army stationed in Boston. These inexperienced soldiers, who did not even have enough supplies, would soon come face-to-face with the best-trained army in the world.

DID YOU KNOW?

George Washington had large joints, massive feet and hands, and problems with his teeth. Washington tried every type of false teeth available at the time, including teeth sold by poor people, wooden teeth, and teeth made from hippopotamus tusks. Nothing made him comfortable.

55

On the morning of June 17, 1775, spectators crowded on rooftops around Boston to watch the British try to remove the militiamen from Breed's Hill. British cannon shots thundered through the sky. The redcoats began to climb the hill, stumbling over rocks and into holes hidden by uncut hay. Meanwhile the soldiers on the hill were ordered to hold their fire while the redcoats came closer and closer.

When the redcoats were within 50 yards (46 meters) of the American defensive line, the colonists opened fire.

British soldiers fell to the ground in droves. The militia deliberately aimed at officers, hoping to cause chaos in the British ranks. However, the redcoats were too disciplined. They regrouped and tried to attack the hill again, but again they were pushed back.

DID YOU KNOW?

Myth tells us that during the Battle of Bunker Hill, an American commander told his men not to fire until they saw the "whites of the enemies' eyes." Actually, this phrase was invented by a writer years after the war. Eighteenth-century muskets were not very accurate. Militiamen let the enemy get within 50 yards before firing so they would not miss their target. However, this was still too far away to see the enemies' eyes.

The British advanced up the hill a third time. By now the colonists were out of gunpowder. They threw rocks at the advancing army. They wielded their muskets like clubs. As British soldiers poured over the **fortifications**, the militia fled.

The battle was finished in two hours. More than 1,000 British soldiers had been killed or wounded. The Americans took 400 casualties. This battle, misnamed the Battle of Bunker Hill, would be the bloodiest clash of the entire war. It was the moment that the British discovered they faced an enemy that was not afraid to fight.

WORDS TO KNOW

fortification: a walled-in area to protect against an enemy.

draft: a government requirement that men join the military.

Hessian: a professional German soldier hired by the British Army.

African American Soldiers

Most African Americans were slaves. Fifty thousand slaves lived in the Northern Colonies and more than 400,000 slaves lived in the South. When the war began, African Americans were faced with a choice: Should they side with the patriots or the British? Black Americans chose the side that offered them the best chance for freedom. Which side do you think that was?

Soldiers For Hire

Not every soldier on the battlefield fought because he felt that it was the right thing to do. Many soldiers simply needed a job. If a colonist was **drafted** but did not want to fight, he could hire a substitute to take his place, usually someone young and poor. The British Army hired mercenaries from Germany, called **Hessians**. A mercenary fights for pay rather than for his country.

enlist: to voluntarily join the military.

WORDS TO KNOW

Some African Americans fought alongside the patriots from the first day of battle. Historical records reveal names of black men who fought at Lexington and Concord, including Peter Salem, Pompy, Prince, and Cato. Some of these men were free and others were slaves whose owners freed them so they could **enlist** in the militia.

When Washington took charge of the Continental Army in 1775, he banned the enlistment of blacks, whether they were slaves or free men. However, when Washington realized that he needed more soldiers, he reversed this policy and allowed free blacks to join the army. Slaves were still banned, although Rhode Island did organize a regiment made up mostly of slaves. These men were promised freedom in exchange for their service. Many slave owners did not want slaves in the army because they feared it might lead to a large-scale slave rebellion. Approximately 5,000 African Americans fought with the patriots during the war.

Many more African Americans fought with the British during the war. Their reason was simple—freedom. In November 1775, Lord Dunmore, the British governor of Virginia, made a proclamation: All slaves who joined the British cause would be freed. Almost 100,000 slaves from the Southern Colonies escaped from their masters and ran to the British lines.

DID YOU KNOW?

Because the Southern Colonies had such a large slave population, they did not want African Americans to serve as soldiers. However, they did recruit them for the navy because sailors did not carry guns. For many blacks, the sea offered the best chance to escape from slavery.

Lord Dunmore

PS

Lord Dunmore convinced African Americans to fight for the British by promising freedom when the war was over. **Read his proclamation.** Do you think he made this offer because he thought it was right or because he needed more soldiers? Do we have enough information to make that choice?

★ ★

A Year of Indecision

Even after the Battle of Bunker Hill, the Second Continental Congress did not yet declare independence from Great Britain. Throughout the fall of 1775, men who wanted to make peace with Britain controlled the Congress. One of those men, John Dickinson of Pennsylvania, wrote the Olive Branch Petition. This letter pleaded with King George to restore the good relationship between the colonies and their mother country. In response, the king announced that he would hire German mercenaries to crush the American rebellion.

While Congress debated whether or not the colonies should declare independence, the war kept growing.

The Continental Army laid **siege** to Boston, where the British had stationed themselves to keep the rebellion down. The British finally abandoned the city in March 1776, and headed to New York in hopes that a victory there would split the colonies in two.

The Continental Congress created a **currency**, bought supplies for the army, and began secret negotiations to get military help from France. But it still did not declare independence! Soon, however, news from the battlefield combined with political propaganda pushed the leaders to the breaking point.

WORDS TO KNOW

siege: when the military surrounds a town or enemy fort and does not allow anything in or out.

currency: a system of money.

59

In the fall of 1775, General Washington ordered Colonel Benedict Arnold and Brigadier General Richard Montgomery to invade Canada, Great Britain's northernmost colony. American soldiers struggled through 200 miles (322 kilometers) of swamps and forests. All their supplies were lost in a hurricane. The men survived on tree bark, candle wax, and their dogs. Arnold arrived in Canada with only 600 of his original 1,100 men.

The British were entrenched in Quebec City, in a fort on a tall cliff above two rivers. Montgomery ordered his men to attack the city on December 31, 1775, in the middle of a snowstorm. It was a complete failure. In three hours, more than one-third of America's colonial army in Canada had been killed. The British lost only 18 men.

WORDS TO KNOW

traitor: someone who is disloyal and abandons or betrays a group or cause.

Hero Turned Traitor

Benedict Arnold is one of the most famous **traitors** in American history, even though early in the war he was considered a hero. However, Arnold did not think he received enough recognition for his deeds. In 1779 he made a secret deal with the British to help them gain control of West Point, which was an important American fort on the Hudson River. The plot was discovered before it could be carried out. Arnold escaped to British lines, where he fought against his country for the rest of the war.

Declaration of Independence

Writer Thomas Paine was born in England but moved to Philadelphia in 1774. As editor of the *Pennsylvania Magazine*, he wrote articles that attacked British policies. In the fall of 1775, some members of the Continental Congress asked Paine to write an essay urging leaders to declare that the colonies were an independent nation.

In a simple, direct style, Paine laid out the logic for American independence in a pamphlet called *Common Sense*. Calling kings "foolish . . . wicked," he argued that if America mended fences with Great Britain, it would forever get a "second hand government." He boldly announced, "'Tis time to part."

WORDS TO KNOW

eloquently: using language clearly and effectively, showing feeling and meaning.

Common Sense ⓅⓈ

Thomas Paine wrote **eloquently** about the conflict between the American colonies and Britain:

"The Sun never shined on a cause of greater worth. 'Tis not the affair of a City, a County, a Province, or a Kingdom; but of a Continent—of at least one-eighth part of the habitable Globe. 'Tis not the concern of a day, a year, or an age; posterity are virtually involved in the contest, and will be more or less affected even to the end of time, by the proceedings now. Now is the seed-time of Continental union, faith and honour."

How does Paine's style of writing contribute to the power of his words?

Common Sense sold thousands of copies. People talked about it in coffee shops and taverns. The seed of independence had been planted and it was sprouting.

On June 7, 1776, Richard Henry Lee stood before the Continental Congress. In a somber tone he proposed a **resolution**. ". . . these United Colonies are . . . free and independent states . . . all political connection between them and the State of Great Britain is . . . totally dissolved."

Finally, Congress would officially vote on the issue that people had been debating for the last year—independence!

Congress created a panel to draft a declaration. Thomas Jefferson wrote most of the document, which was read before the entire Congress. After debating on it and revising the wording, the vote was cast on July 2. Should the 13 colonies announce to the world that they were a free and self-governing country? New York did not vote, but the other 12 colonies voted yes.

WORDS TO KNOW

resolution: a firm decision to do or not do something.

Thomas Jefferson: Slave-Owning Lover of Liberty

In the Declaration of Independence, Thomas Jefferson wrote, "all men are created equal," and was upset when statements against slavery were taken out of his first draft of the document. Jefferson had described slavery as a "cruel war against human nature itself." However, he owned at least 600 slaves during the course of his life. At Monticello, his Virginia plantation, Jefferson ran a nail factory where slave boys were whipped when they did not work fast enough. Jefferson may have been morally opposed to slavery, but his lifestyle depended upon it.

A Break-Up Letter: The Declaration of Independence (PS)

Have you ever ended a friendship with someone because that person hurt you? When the Americans decided to break up with Great Britain, they wanted the world to know why. The Declaration of Independence states that " . . . all men are created equal . . . they are **endowed** by their Creator with certain **unalienable** Rights . . . among these are Life, Liberty and the **pursuit** of Happiness." The Americans believed that all people should have life, liberty, and happiness. The declaration lists all the ways King George III had denied these rights to the colonists. Read the Declaration of Independence. Did the Americans have good reasons for breaking up with Great Britain?

John Adams predicted that in the future, July 2 would be celebrated with "pomp and parade, with shews [shows], games, guns, bells bonfires . . . from one end of this continent to the other from this time forward forever more." Adams got it almost right. The Declaration of Independence was formally approved on July 4, so this is the day Americans celebrate as Independence Day.

WORDS TO KNOW

endowed: to be given something.

unalienable: something that cannot be taken away.

pursuit: to try to catch something.

DID YOU KNOW?

Less than 50 percent of the English public supported the tough Coercive Acts. In 1775, Parliament was bombarded with petitions and protests from the English. Why do you think Britain went ahead with the war when so many British people disapproved of it? Are there any recent conflicts when the populations of the countries involved didn't want war?

THESIS STATEMENT

Now it's time to interpret what you have read in this chapter and answer the Essential Question:

What caused American leaders to finally declare independence in July 1776? How would our country today be different without the Declaration of Independence?

ACTIVITY

Build Your Own Artillery

Supplies: *plastic spoon, tape, marshmallows, measuring tape, raisins, dried beans*

Both the British and Continental armies relied on artillery, which are large guns fired from a distance. The three types of Revolutionary War artillery were cannons, mortars, and howitzers. Test your artillery skills with a spoon cannon and a marshmallow cannon ball.

1 Tape the handle of the spoon to the edge of a table so the spoon is facing up.

2 With one hand hold a marshmallow in the spoon. Use your other hand to anchor the spoon where it's taped.

3 Bend the spoon back and release it. Measure how far your marshmallow flies.

4 Place a target on the floor and see if you can hit it. How can you reposition the spoon to make the marshmallow fly higher or farther? Keep track of your measurements on a chart.

TRY THIS: What happens if you fire a raisin or a bean? Do the objects fly farther if they weigh less? What other household items can you use to make a more sophisticated cannon?

Sew Your Own Ditty Bag

Supplies: *old pair of jeans, scissors, washable marker, ruler, needle, thread, straight pins, safety pin, shoestring, decorations*

Sailors were skilled sewers because they had to repair ship sails. They sewed ditty bags to carry their personal possessions.

1 Cut an 8-inch section (20 centimeters) off one leg of the jeans. Turn this section inside out.

2 Mark a line 1 inch (2½ centimeters) from one of the open edges of the leg. Pin the two sides of the leg together along this line. Use small stitches to sew this seam together.

3 Mark a line 1-inch line (2½ centimeters) along the opposite, open edge. Cut a slit along one seam from the edge to the line. Fold the material back to the line. Pin and sew this seam. This is the sleeve for the tie for your bag.

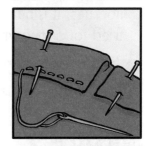

4 Attach a safety pin to one end of the shoestring. Thread the string through the sleeve. Remove the safety pin and tie knots in both ends of the shoestring.

5 Turn the bag right side out and decorate it!

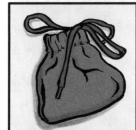

ACTIVITY

Write Your Own Preamble in Slang

Supplies: *pencil, paper*

The Declaration of Independence contains three parts. The preamble sums up the principles that American liberty is based upon. The second section lists 28 complaints against King George. The final section announces that the colonies are free and independent. What might the preamble sound like if it were written in slang?

WORDS TO KNOW

preamble: an introduction.

1 Compare the summary of the preamble found below, to the original text of the preamble.

We believe that all people are born with the rights of life, liberty, and the pursuit of happiness. The people create governments to protect these rights. When governments try to take these rights away, the people have the right to repair or replace the government. We should not change governments for unimportant reasons. But when a government keeps taking away our liberties, it is our right and duty to change the government. King George has tried for a long time to take away American liberties.

2 Use modern slang to explain why colonists no longer want to be part of Great Britain. Below are a few ideas.

* King George, you aren't the boss of me now.
* Hey, G.B., we're outta here.
* Uh, Parliament, hey guys, we've totally gotta go. Wanna know why?

Make Your Own Quill Pen

Supplies: *large feather, rag, scissors, toothpick, ½ cup (118 milliliters) blueberries, strainer, wooden spoon, bowl, writing paper*

John Hancock was the first person to sign the Declaration of Independence. Today, when people tell you to "put your John Hancock here," they are asking for your signature. Most people in the 1700s used pens made from goose feathers. Make your own quill pen and practice your John Hancock.

1 Use the rag to brush dust and dirt from the feather.

2 Hold the feather like a pen. If any feathers get in the way of your grip, trim these off with the scissors.

3 Cut the fat end of the feather at an angle to make a sharp point. Clean out the tip of the feather with the toothpick.

4 Put the blueberries in a strainer and set the strainer on top of a large bowl. Use the wooden spoon to mash the berries against the strainer until juice drains into the bowl. This is your ink.

5 Carefully dip the quill into the berry ink. Gently shake off the extra ink and write on the paper.

Chapter 5
The Grim Tides of War

Through the summer of 1776, the Continental Army waited nervously on Manhattan and Long Island in New York for the British to attack. The British invasion force floated in New York Harbor, growing bigger every day. By August, 70 British ships, hundreds of boats, and 32,000 redcoats were ready to attack. If the British captured New York, they would split the Northern Colonies from the colonies in the south.

? ESSENTIAL QUESTION

Why did soldiers and civilians remain with the army even under terrible conditions?

General Washington's defenses were strong, except for a little-known trail on Long Island that no one was guarding. On the night of August 26, General Henry Clinton led thousands of redcoats through the unguarded pass. The next morning, Hessian artillery from German mercenaries bombarded the Americans while Clinton's soldiers attacked from the rear, surrounding the colonists. The savage fighting lasted all day.

General Washington watched the action from a hill. At one point he cried, "Good God, what brave fellows I must this day lose!"

And lose he did. Three thousand soldiers were killed and more than 1,000 were taken prisoner. The British lost only 59 redcoats and

five Hessians. Altogether, more than 40,000 men fought in the Battle of New York in a crushing defeat for the colonists.

General William Howe, the commander in charge of British forces, ordered his men to cease fire as night fell. This was Washington's chance. He ordered his men to leave their campfires lit and muffle their wagon

wheels with rags. All night, in complete silence, 9,000 troops marched to the Hudson River and ferried across to Manhattan Island. The next morning, when the British resumed the attack on the Americans, they discovered the enemy had vanished.

What if General Howe had kept firing on American soldiers and won the war? Would you be a British citizen or an American one?

By early December the Continental Army had abandoned New York and fled across New Jersey. The Revolutionary War had barely begun and already the rebels were on the verge of defeat.

"These Are the Times That Try Men's Souls"

On December 8, 1776, the British Army followed hot on the heels of the Continental Army. The American soldiers needed to get out of New Jersey and find safety in Pennsylvania. Snow covered the ground and men shivered as they struggled to get their horses and artillery into boats so they could cross the ice-clogged Delaware River. Charles Willson Peale, a Philadelphia militiaman, described the scene as "the most hellish . . . I ever beheld."

The army that disembarked on the Pennsylvania side of the river was a ragged collection of 3,000 men. Their ranks had been shrinking since the disastrous defeat in New York. Soldiers refused to reenlist after their time expired, and hundreds more simply deserted. The remaining troops were sick, hungry, and miserable.

Knowing that most of their enlistments were set to expire on December 31, Washington despaired. Washington wrote to his brother that if more soldiers were not recruited soon, ". . . I think the game is pretty near up."

DID YOU KNOW?

Thomas Paine was a soldier in the Continental Army in December 1776. Later he wrote an essay called *The Crisis*, describing the qualities he witnessed in his fellow soldiers. "These are the times that try men's souls. The summer soldier and the sunshine patriot will . . . shrink from the service of his country; but he that stands it now, deserves the love and thanks of man and woman."

General Howe did not pursue Washington's ragged army into Pennsylvania. Instead, he retired to New York to wait out the winter. General Washington, however, could not wait for spring. He needed a victory.

WORDS TO KNOW

barracks: housing for soldiers.

A troop of Hessians guarded the New Jersey side of the Delaware River. They were stationed in **barracks** in the town of Trenton. Washington concocted a bold plan.

Early on Christmas morning, he gathered 2,400 men along the river landing. Many of the men's boots had split open—a bloody trail in the snow marked where they walked. The freezing temperatures dropped even lower. The river's current was swift, the wind strong, and ice floes blocked a clear path through the water. Despite these obstacles, all the men, their horses, and the artillery were ferried across the river.

Safety on Board

The design on the New Jersey quarter features General Washington crossing the Delaware River. The engraving is based on a painting made by Emanuel Gottlieb Leutze and shows Washington standing in the front of a boat. Is this painting historically accurate? What might have happened to Washington if he'd really spent the journey like that? Why do you think the artist portrayed him standing?

After landing, they trudged 9 miles (14 kilometers) to Trenton in driving sleet. Washington was told that the gunpowder was wet from the sleet. He replied, "Use the bayonet. I am resolved to take Trenton." The exhausted Continental Army attacked the Hessian barracks just after dawn, and in less than an hour the battle was over.

The exhausted, but victorious, army crossed the river again—this time accompanied by 918 Hessian prisoners of war.

On December 30, General Washington stood before his men and made a speech, something he rarely did. He told the men that they had done more than their share. But, he said, ". . . we know not how to spare you." He told them, "Your country is at stake, your wives, your houses and all that you hold dear."

There was a long silence after the general's speech. Finally, one old veteran stepped forward to say he could not go home as long as his country still needed him. More men followed the veteran's lead and 1,200 Continental soldiers reenlisted. Washington collected his army to attack Princeton.

During the Battle of Princeton, Washington rode at the front lines. Bullets whizzed around his prancing horse, but Washington did not flee or duck. Instead, he urged his men forward as the British line fell apart.

Washington galloped after the British yelling, "It's a fine fox chase, boys!"

With the two back-to-back victories of Trenton and Princeton, American **morale** soared. But the war was far from over.

WORDS TO **KNOW**

morale: feelings of enthusiasm and loyalty that a person or group has about a task or job.

Capital Capture and Saratoga Surrender

What better way to destroy your enemy than strike him in the heart? In September 1777 British General Howe did just that by capturing Philadelphia, America's largest capital.

The Continental Congress, which governed from Philadelphia, was forced to flee when the British arrived. The British Army settled in for a cozy winter in decent quarters where they'd stay fairly warm. Washington and the Continental Army, however, had to retreat to their crude camp at Valley Forge, Pennsylvania, for the winter.

DID YOU KNOW?

Burgoyne's plan was to march along Lake Champlain and the Hudson River to Albany, New York, and cut off New England from the rest of the states.

Not all news was bleak for the colonies in the fall of 1777. British General John Burgoyne, also known as "Gentleman Johnny," had invaded the northern states in June. He led an army of 7,000 British, Hessian, Canadian, Native American, and Tory troops south from Canada.

Seventy miles (113 kilometers) from Albany, New York, the hilly American wilderness stopped them. The British wagons could not get through the thick forest. American troops, led by Horatio Gates, were determined to prevent Burgoyne from reaching Albany.

The Americans dug in on Bemis Heights, where the Hudson River flows past high bluffs. Burgoyne decided to cross the Hudson River and fight the Americans. The two armies clashed on September 19, when Burgoyne attacked colonial soldiers at a clearing called Freeman's Farm. The American

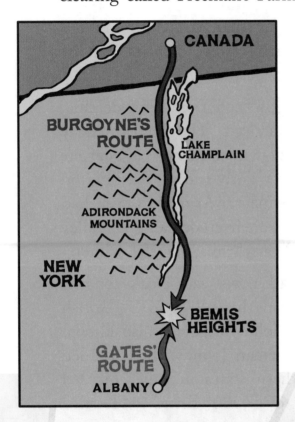

defenses were too strong, and the British fell back. Burgoyne decided to wait for General Howe to send reinforcements. He waited and waited, but no reinforcements came.

Burgoyne tried to break through the American line a second time. He failed again and withdrew to the village of Saratoga, New York. Meanwhile, militia from nearby towns flocked to Gates' army. The American forces swelled to 17,000 men, and on October 17, 1777, the British Army at Saratoga surrendered.

DID YOU KNOW?

Not all Germans fought for the British. Baron von Friedrich Steuben trained the Continental Army at Valley Forge. He was famous for shouting orders in both German and French with English swear words sprinkled in.

World War

News of the victory at Saratoga convinced the French that the time was ripe for France to enter this war against its old British enemy. France hoped to gain back some of the land it had lost in 1763. Soon Spain and Holland followed France's lead. The American Revolution had become a world war.

Winter Camp at Valley Forge

Throughout the bitter winter of 1777, the Continental Army huddled in tents and lean-tos in the hills of Valley Forge. There were not enough tents, clothes, blankets, or food because the Continental Congress had no power to tax the states and raise money for supplies. Many loyalist farmers and merchants sold their goods to the British instead of the colonists.

The troops at Valley Forge struggled. Ebenezer Wild, a soldier from Massachusetts, recalled surviving for days on "a leg of nothing."

Soldiers hunted for any food they could find. Many stole from orchards and farms around camp.

Soldiers admitted that sometimes they took food from citizens at the point of a bayonet—they were desperately hungry.

On average, 10 men deserted daily from Valley Forge. Washington also reported that he had to suppress a "dangerous **mutiny**" on December 23, 1777. A soldier named Joseph Plumb Martin wrote that, even though the men ". . . were truly patriotic, they loved their country . . . but to starve to death was too much . . . ." Twenty-five percent of the soldiers who wintered at Valley Forge died.

WORDS TO KNOW

mutiny: a rebellion of soldiers against their commanding officer.

Women on the Battle Front

Thousands of wives, widows, and runaway servants followed the Continental Army from battle to battle. They worked as cooks, washerwomen, and nurses. Some followed the army to be close to their husbands, others to earn a living. While the army depended on the labor of these women, they also slowed the army down. These camp followers suffered the same hardships as soldiers—hunger, disease, discomfort, and danger. Many women brought their children, even babies, to war with them.

DID YOU KNOW? Deborah Sampson dressed like a man, called herself Robert Shurtleff, and enlisted in the army. She served for 17 months before being discovered.

Between 3,000 and 7,000 women were camp followers during the Revolutionary War.

Some women even became legends. In the sweltering summer of 1778, the Continental and British armies clashed near Monmouth Courthouse in New Jersey. At the end of the day, Americans held the field.

From the debris of the battle rose the legend of "Molly Pitcher." Stories swirled about the wife of a Continental soldier who carried water to soldiers and took charge of her husband's cannon when he was killed. Today, historians believe that this courageous woman was Mary Ludwig Hays McCauley.

Women Spies

Both the Americans and British used female spies. Anna Smith Strong worked with the Culper Spy Ring in New York. She used the laundry on her clothesline to send clues to her fellow patriots about British troop movements. Ann Bates, a loyalist teacher in Philadelphia, disguised herself as a peddler and sold needles, thread, and knives to the Continental Army while gathering information for the British. Why do you think female spies attracted little attention?

pension: an amount of money paid at regular times for past service.

WORDS TO KNOW

The requirements to join the Continental Army were simple: male, "able-bodied," and capable of pulling a trigger. Since soldiers did not often bathe or change clothes, women could dress like men and join up. There is historical evidence of several women who fought in the war, served honorably, and received military **pensions** afterward.

Because female soldiers disguised their gender, there were probably many female soldiers whose names were never recorded. It is likely that their heroism will remain a mystery.

The Native Americans' War

The Declaration of Independence states that Great Britain had unleashed the "merciless Indian savages" on the people of the frontier. In fact, most Native Americans were neutral when the war began. However, as fighting raged through the countryside, more Native Americans joined the British. They felt that the American colonists posed a greater threat to their land and liberty than a king who lived 3,000 miles away (4,828 kilometers).

The Iroquois League was made up of six tribes in the Northeast that had long allied with each other. This cooperation shattered when the tribes joined different sides in the war. The Oneidas and Tuscaroras served as scouts for the Continental Army. The Mohawks, Onondagas, Cayugas, and Senecas fought with the British.

DID YOU KNOW?

After the war, the United States took over all the land east of the Mississippi. Thousands of Native Americans lived on this land but the U.S. government did not recognize their rights. Many of them migrated to Canada to seek a better life.

In 1779, General John Sullivan led Continental soldiers into Iroquois lands in central New York to destroy homes and food. Fifteen thousand bushels of corn, beans, squash, and potatoes were torched. Fruit orchards were burned and **livestock** slaughtered. That winter, many Iroquois starved or froze to death. The war was a painful sign that the Native American way of life would continue to be affected by the Europeans, who had arrived nearly 300 years earlier.

WORDS TO KNOW

livestock: animals raised for food and other uses.

? THESIS STATEMENT

Now it's time to interpret what you have read in this chapter and answer the Essential Question:

Why did soldiers and civilians remain with the army even under terrible conditions?

Make Your Own Invisible Ink

Supplies: *2 tablespoons baking soda, 2 tablespoons water, bowl, spoon or whisk, cotton swabs, unlined white paper, cup of purple grape juice, paintbrush (see chart in glossary for metric equivalents)*

Sometimes spies used invisible ink in case their messages fell into enemy hands. The ink was made from a combination of sulfate and water. When the letter was held over a flame, the writing appeared.

1 Mix the baking soda and water together to make a thin paste.

2 Use a cotton swab dipped in the paste to write a message on the paper. Let it dry.

3 When you are ready to reveal your message, paint over the paper with grape juice. The chemical reaction produces a color change so the message becomes visible.

The Culper Spy Ring

The Culper Spy Ring formed in 1778 to pass information about the British troops. The spies used a secret code based on numbers to share what the British were doing, where they were going, and how they could be disrupted. You can use the same code as the revolutionary spies to create your own secret messages!

ACTIVITY

Guess Your Own Cure For Sickness

Most eighteenth-century doctors learned on the job. At the time, people did not know that germs spread disease. They had no anesthesia to put a patient to sleep before surgery.

1 Match the ailment on the left with its correct treatment on the right. Check your matches against correct answers on the next page.

Ailment	Cure
Fever	Break apart some ripe puff-balls. Save the powder and put this on the body.
Asthma	Rub your head for 15 minutes.
A bleeding limb after an amputation	Drink the juice of radishes.
Blistered feet	Boil a chicken for one hour in two gallons of water. Then drink the water.
Burn	Thread a needle and draw it through the skin. Leave the thread in place until the skin falls off.
Vomiting	Mix 25 drops of liquid lead with a pint of rainwater and apply to skin.
Head cold	Lay roasted turnips behind your ear.
Headache	Take six pills made of cobwebs before you get the chills.
Toothache	Peel the rind of an orange. Slice it thin and roll it inside out. Slide one roll into each nostril.

* **Fever:** Take six pills made of cobwebs before you get the chills.

* **Asthma:** Drink the juice of radishes.

* **A bleeding limb after an amputation:** Break apart some ripe puff-balls. Save the powder and put this on the wound.

* **Blistered feet:** Thread a needle and draw it through the skin. Leave the thread in place until the skin falls off.

* **Burn:** Mix 25 drops of liquid lead with a pint of rainwater and apply to skin.

* **Vomiting:** Boil a chicken for one hour in two gallons of water. Then drink the water.

* **Head cold:** Peel the rind of an orange. Slice it thin and roll it inside out. Slide one roll into each nostril.

* **Headache:** Rub your head for 15 minutes.

* **Toothache:** Lay roasted turnips behind your ear.

DID YOU KNOW?

American soldiers had a 2 percent chance of dying on the battlefield, but that death rate leaped to 25 percent if a soldier was hospitalized!

Gunther's Disease

King George III suffered from an illness that may have influenced his behavior. His urine was pink and his teeth were stained red. He had a rash on his body and sometimes seemed insane. Historians believe the king suffered from Gunther's disease, a rare disease where normal body chemicals accumulate in toxic amounts. Gunther's disease causes severe pain, confusion and seizures, and blistering of the skin from sun exposure.

ACTIVITY

Cook Your Own Firecake

Supplies: *1 cup flour, 1 teaspoon salt, bowl, water, mixing spoon, cookie sheet, cooking oil, paper towel, oven (see chart in glossary for metric equivalents)*

When soldiers were on the march, they made their bread at the end of the day. The troops only had flour and water and, if they were lucky, a little salt. Soldiers called this bread firecakes. They cooked it over coals on a flat rock or a piece of wood. CAUTION: Ask an adult for help with the oven.

1 Mix flour and salt together in a bowl. Add water one tablespoon at a time. The dough should form a ball and be the consistency of Play-Doh.

2 Grease the cookie sheet with a little cooking oil on a paper towel.

3 Break off golf ball–size pieces of dough and press them flat. Place the cakes on a greased cookie sheet, spreading them out so they are not touching.

4 Bake your firecakes at 400 degrees Fahrenheit (204 degrees Celsius) for 12 minutes. How do they taste?

DID YOU KNOW? ★ ★ ★ ★ ★ ★ ★ ★

Sarah Osborn cooked for the army during the war. When she applied for a government pension, she explained why her role had been important. "It would not do for men to fight and starve too."

Chapter 6
Everyday Life During War

Eliza Wilkinson heard horses galloping up the path to her door. Men bellowed horrible curses and Eliza's heart chilled. Before she could flee, redcoats burst into her house, their swords and pistols drawn. "Where're these women rebels?" they shouted. They split open trunks and took Eliza's clothing, even the buckles on her shoes! They left with their shirts stuffed with stolen goods.

privateer: a privately owned ship that the government paid to capture enemy vessels.

WORDS TO KNOW

? **ESSENTIAL QUESTION**

How did the war impact civilian life? Was this fair?

The British Against the War

The longer the war lasted, the less support people in Great Britain felt toward it. Ireland was part of the Britain Empire, and many Irish people sympathized with the colonists. They too felt they were treated unfairly by Parliament. Irish leaders organized their own boycotts and militia. To avoid another rebellion, Parliament acted quickly and gave Ireland more freedom to trade and more political freedom. This satisfied Ireland enough to remain in the empire for the time being.

The war was costing the British government a fortune, and British citizens living in England, Scotland, and Wales had to pay the bill. They were taxed on everything: stamps, newspapers, and even the rabbit hair used on women's hats!

British merchants also hated the war. They had grown rich on trade with America, and with the onset of war, that trade dried up. Plus, merchant ships were often captured by the American navy and by **privateers**. As a result, prices of both livestock and land in England plummeted.

The British military had to cope with the problem of getting enough men to enlist in the military. Parliament hired Hessians to staff the army, but they used press gangs to get more sailors. A press gang was a group of thugs who seized men off the street and forced them onto ships headed for America.

DID YOU KNOW?

The Revolutionary War touched the lives of people all over the world, far from the battlefield.

As news of battlefield defeats hit the British newspapers, families worried about their sons dying in a land far away.

Do you think lack of British support is one reason Britain lost the war?

Women's Roles

Regardless of whether they were loyalists or patriots, American women on the home front worked hard during the war. They had no choice—with the men off fighting, women were left to do all the chores, including the work that the men usually took care of.

A typical colonial woman baked bread, preserved vegetables, cured meat, cooked and cleaned up meals, made candles, hand-washed laundry, spun thread, sewed clothes, cleaned house, cared for the children, served as the family teacher and doctor, and more. Now women also had to plant and harvest crops, cut and haul firewood, repair fences, forge tools, and butcher animals. The work never ended.

Temperance Smith, a preacher's wife from Connecticut, could not even settle long enough to pray for her husband's safety. She worried whether she had remembered "to set the sponge [yeast] for the bread, put water on the leach tub, turn the cloth in the dying vat, chopped enough wood for kindling . . . ." And on and on. She told the story of her own American Revolution experience to her three children, who later published the story in a magazine.

How does a first-hand account of ordinary life help us better understand the war?

Women were not allowed to vote in the 1700s, but they voiced their political opinions in other ways. When the boycott against British imports began, women across New England joined patriotic spinning bees. Instead of buying British cloth, they made their own. Eleven-year-old Anna Winslow from Boston called herself a "daughter of liberty" when she learned how to spin wool into yarn. Women signed petitions in which they pledged not to drink tea until the tea tax was repealed. Newspapers reported a group of women in New Hampshire who "made their breakfast upon rye coffee."

PS   American Poet

Phillis Wheatley was captured in Africa at the age of 7 and sold into slavery. Her owners in America taught Phillis how to read and write. Her first poem was published when she was only 13. Wheatley wrote more than 100 poems during her lifetime. Some of the poems reveal her love for America, while others condemn the practice of slavery. Here she expresses hope that the new earl of Dartmouth will improve things for African Americans.

No more, America, in mournful strain
Of wrongs, and grievance unredress'd complain,
No longer shalt thou dread the iron chain,
Which wanton Tyranny with lawless hand
Had made, and with it meant t' enslave the land.

Betsy Ross—History or Myth?

Most schoolchildren are taught that a seamstress named Betsy Ross made the first American flag. In 1870, Betsy Ross's grandson published a story that claimed his grandmother had designed the flag for General Washington when he stopped by her shop in 1776. But there is no evidence to prove this is true! Ross was an upholsterer who stuffed mattresses, made curtains, and covered chairs. She did sew flags, but we may never know for certain if she designed the Stars and Stripes.

Women also began to think about the meaning of **equality**. In 1776, Abigail Adams wrote a letter to her husband, John Adams, who was at the Continental Congress helping Thomas Jefferson write the Declaration of Independence. Abigail wrote, "I desire you would remember the ladies. . . . Do not put such unlimited power in the hands of the Husbands . . . we . . . will not hold ourselves bound by any laws in which we have no voice, or representation."

equality: being treated the same, with the same rights and opportunities as others.

WORDS TO KNOW

DID YOU KNOW?

Women did not get the right to vote in the United States until 1920.

Poor women showed their political views in a more rowdy way—they rioted! Between 1776 and 1779, citizens rioted more than 30 times to confront merchants they thought were guilty of hiking up the price of scarce goods. In 1776, a New York merchant refused to sell the tea in his storehouse for a reasonable price. The town women stormed the warehouse, opened the tea chests, weighed and packaged the tea, and sold it to themselves.

inflation: a continuing rise in the price of goods and services.

barter: to trade goods without relying on money.

WORDS TO KNOW

Part of the reason women found cause to riot was **inflation**. Paying the bills was a challenge for the Continental Congress. The Congress created a national currency called Continentals. The money was issued in the amount of a dollar or fractions of a dollar. However, when too many Continentals were printed, the prices of goods increased. This is called inflation.

Jon Boucher was a schoolteacher in Virginia before the Revolutionary War. His yearly salary was $4,000 in today's money. A good horse saddle cost $180 and a wig (which most men wore) about $145. A pound of butter cost $1.50 and a prayer book $13.50. These prices show that the average colonist did not have much money for luxuries.

DID YOU KNOW?

A new saying was born. If someone wanted to describe something as worthless, he would say, "It ain't worth a Continental." Many merchants used the **barter** method instead of accepting Continentals for payment. After the war, the dollar was established as the United States' official currency. Later, dimes and pennies were created.

Dollar for Dollar

Find out what your family pays for a pound of butter or a book. How do the prices compare? What does this tell you about inflation today?

The Loyalist Experience

Historians estimate that 20 percent of colonists remained loyal to Great Britain during the war. Sometimes even family members chose different sides. Benjamin Franklin was an innovator and politician who served in the Constitutional Convention. He was a diplomat to France and one of the men who signed the Declaration of Independence. Meanwhile, his son William was a loyalist who was arrested for treason and imprisoned in a dungeon 70 feet (21 meters) below ground. His father did not lift a finger to help him.

After 1781, the British Army began to withdraw from American cities. This was a terrifying time for loyalists. Their neighbors thought they were traitors and wanted revenge.

Some people, who were desperate to escape, scurried on board British ships. Other families stood on the street, wringing their hands, as they tried to decide if they should flee or stay. Loyalists who stayed were arrested and thrown into dungeons. Others were **tarred and feathered** or forced to wear the label "Tory."

Loyalists were thrown out of their homes and forced to sleep in the street.

Native American Tory

The Iroquois was an alliance of Native Americans that included Mohawk Chief Thayendanegea, also known as Joseph Brant. Worried that American colonists wanted Indian lands, Brant became a Tory. As a British commander, he led raids against patriots in New York. When the British lost the war, the Iroquois followed Brant to Canada, a land still ruled by the British.

After the war ended, approximately 60,000 loyalists left the country. Hannah Ingraham was only 11 when her family left New York for Nova Scotia. She said, "It was a sad sick time after we landed . . . . We had to live in tents . . . the melting snow and the rain would soak up in our beds as we lay. Mother got so chilled and . . . was never well afterwards."

Most loyalists settled in Canada. Some went to the British colonies in the Caribbean Islands, while others moved to England. Many recorded their aching homesickness for the country they had left behind. James Clarke, a loyalist who moved to Nova Scotia, wrote to a friend that his love of Rhode Island was so strong he would ". . . freely give up my Life and Ten Thousand more . . ." if he could go back to how things used to be.

?

THESIS STATEMENT

Now it's time to interpret what you have read in this chapter and answer the Essential Question:

How did the war impact civilian life? Was this fair?

Play Your Own Revolutionary War Game

Supplies: *4 or more players, one small stick for each player*

Even in the midst of war, children found time to play. With no video games or television, children relied on their imaginations. Slave children on plantations played games such as this one that came from West Africa.

1 All players sit in a circle with their sticks in front of them.

2 Memorize the following saying: Sae' sae' brae wah a deisha. The words are pronounced like this: "Sa sa bray wah ah deesha."

3 All players recite the phrase together as they pick up their sticks and set them in front of the person on their right. Keep reciting and passing the stick, first slowly and then faster and faster. Each time a player mispronounces the saying or does not pass the stick properly, he is out of the circle. The last person in the circle is the winner.

TRY THIS: Today, people still play many games that originated in Africa. Research online to find these games and try them out in your home. Ask an adult before you use the Internet.

ACTIVITY

Cook Your Own Indian Pudding

Supplies: *oven and stove, saucepan and spoon, 2 cups milk, 1¼ cups cornmeal, whisk, 3 tablespoons melted butter, 6 tablespoons sugar, 1½ teaspoons each ground cinnamon, nutmeg, and cloves, 6 tablespoons raisins, mixing bowl, 3 eggs, 2 tablespoons cream, greased 9-inch pie plate, butter knife (see chart in glossary for metric equivalents)*

Indian pudding was a common treat made from basic ingredients. CAUTION: Ask an adult for help when you use the stove.

1 Preheat oven to 360 degrees Fahrenheit (182 degrees Celsius).

2 In a saucepan, stir the milk over medium heat for two minutes.

3 Remove the pan from the heat, slowly whisk in the cornmeal, and return the pan to medium heat until thick. Remove the pan from heat. Add melted butter, sugar, spices, and raisins and blend thoroughly.

4 In a mixing bowl, whisk the eggs and cream. Add this to the cornmeal mixture and stir well.

5 Pour the mixture into a greased 9-inch pie plate and bake for 30 minutes or until a knife stuck in the center comes out clean.

TRY THIS: How does Indian pudding taste compared to treats today? Is it as sweet? Why or why not?

Chapter 7
Victory at Last

★ ★

The ragged line of men stared at their new
commander. Major General Nathanael Greene was not
like their previous commanders. He was plump and
walked with a limp. Instead of the fire of a military
leader, Greene radiated a calm confidence.

stalemate: a contest where neither side is winning.

WORDS TO KNOW

? ESSENTIAL QUESTION

How did General Washington's decision to march his army to Yorktown affect the outcome of the war? Do you consider him a good general?

Greene stared back at the rag-tag group of 2,000 soldiers he had been sent to lead in North Carolina. Many wore no shoes. Their feet were wrapped in rags. They shivered and sniffed and many looked barely able to carry a musket.

With the war in the North at a **stalemate** in the fall of 1778, the British had headed south. By 1780 they had captured the key port cities of Savannah, Georgia, and Charleston, South Carolina. Then, in August, British General Charles Cornwallis dealt the colonists a harsh blow at the Battle of Camden in South Carolina.

General Washington needed a commander in the South that he could rely on.

Nathanael Greene did not want the job. He was a New England man and he wanted to spend the winter with his wife and children in Rhode Island. But Greene obeyed his commander-in-chief and went to the Carolinas. There, Greene saw an opportunity and seized it.

The Road to Yorktown

Greene knew his small army could not defeat the British in a face-off, so he made an unusual decision. He divided the army. He ordered Brigadier General Daniel Morgan to go west with a detachment of troops.

Morgan's men were pursued by Lieutenant Colonel Banastre Tarleton. Tarleton was nicknamed "Bloody Ben" because in an earlier battle his soldiers had killed colonial soldiers after they had surrendered. Tarleton pushed his soldiers over tough terrain and through flooded rivers. The exhausted British caught up to the militiamen on January 16, 1781, in a grazing area known as Cowpens, South Carolina.

Letter Home

PS

Nathanael Greene wrote many letters home to his wife during the war. What information can historians find in personal letters from certain time periods? Why is this important? What does it add to our knowledge about different wars?

"You can have no idea of the distress and misery that prevails in this quarter. Hundreds of families that formerly livd in great opulence are now reducd to beggary and want. A Gentleman from Georgia was this morning with me, to get assistance to move his wife and family out of the Enemies way. They have been separated for upwards of eight months, during all which time the wife never heard from her husband, nor the husband from his wife. Her distress was so great that she has been obligd to sell all her plate, table linnen and even wearing apparel, to maintain her poor little children."

At one point in the battle, British troops thought a unit of Virginia militiamen was withdrawing. Instead, the men wheeled about and fired a volley straight into the British line only 30 yards away. Then they charged with fixed bayonets. The British ran. At the end of the day, 76 percent of Tarleton's men were dead or wounded.

Despite the defeat at Cowpens, British control in the South expanded.

The British commander in charge of the Southern campaign was General Charles Cornwallis. He won many victories, but could not pin Greene's army down long enough to destroy it. Meanwhile, French troops led by General Rochambeau had reinforced General Washington's army in the North. They gathered in New York to attack the British forces, which were led by General Henry Clinton.

DID YOU KNOW?

During the French and Indian War, Daniel Morgan was charged with disobeying a British officer and sentenced to 500 lashes. Morgan claimed that the soldier who whipped him only gave him 499. Before the Battle of Cowpens, he showed his men the gruesome sight of the scars on his back to rile them up for battle.

The War at Sea

There was basically no Continental Navy during the war. Great Britain ruled the seas until the French joined the war in 1778. Then Spain and Holland declared war on Great Britain too. Even the British Royal Navy was no match for the combined fleets of four enemies. The Continental Congress hired privateers to attack British ships, but privateers were motivated by profit instead of patriotism. The captain and crew divided the wealth confiscated from each ship seized.

Clinton prepared for the attack. He also sent orders to Cornwallis to build a naval base in Virginia. By early fall, Cornwallis and 7,000 British soldiers had dug in on the Chesapeake Peninsula at Yorktown, Virginia.

Washington plotted how best to attack Clinton's army in New York. He needed naval support to win, but America had no navy to speak of. Then, on August 14, 1781, Washington received good news. A French fleet of 28 ships commanded by Admiral Francois Joseph Paul de Grasse was sailing for the Chesapeake.

Here was the navy Washington needed—but it was not headed for New York!

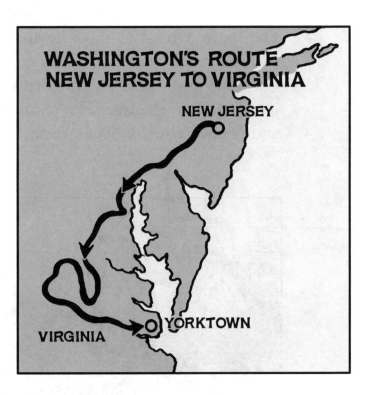

Washington changed plans. He decided to march to Yorktown and trap Cornwallis's army. The success of this plan depended on coordination and deception. Washington needed a head start, so General Clinton couldn't know the colonists were headed south.

Washington ordered troops in New Jersey to build baker's ovens, since an army that baked bread surely was not going anywhere. On August 19, American and French soldiers pretended to march toward the camp with the ovens. Then they pivoted southwest. Marching double-time, the army hiked 15 miles (24 kilometers) a day on the 500-mile march (805 kilometers) to Yorktown.

Remember, this was an age without cell phones. Bridges were practically nonexistent and roads were little more than trails. For Washington's plan to succeed, two armies had to coordinate with a French admiral. One army spoke English, the other army spoke French, and the admiral was somewhere in the Atlantic Ocean. These three forces had to unite before Clinton caught on and sent reinforcements from New York.

What were the chances of success?

Fortune was on America's side. Admiral de Grasse and the French fleet reached the Chesapeake Bay before the British Navy, so the French admiral was able to position his ships strategically. On September 5, 1781, the British and French fought the largest naval battle of the war. The outnumbered British fleet was mangled and limped back to New York.

Meanwhile, Cornwallis ordered his men to build large fortifications around Yorktown. Then they hunkered down to wait for General Clinton to send reinforcements. On September 28, the British heard the thud of thousands of marching feet, but it wasn't the reinforcements they were waiting for.

The Continental Army and its French allies had arrived.

Ten British **redoubts** ringed Yorktown. These ditches were 6 feet deep (almost 2 meters) and 16 feet wide (almost 5 meters), lined with sharpened sticks to snag enemy soldiers. Cannons and howitzers were mounted on platforms in the redoubts.

Washington ordered men to work at night to dig a series of trenches close to the British redoubts where artillerymen could position their guns. On October 9, the Americans and the French began to bombard Yorktown 24 hours a day, seven days a week. Under siege, life in the town became impossible. Houses were bombed to rubble and dead bodies lay everywhere. Disease spread throughout the British camp. But Cornwallis still did not surrender, certain that General Clinton's reinforcements would arrive.

The thought of those reinforcements worried Washington and Rochambeau. They had captured all the redoubts except numbers nine and ten. These had to be taken so they could shoot a clear line of fire directly into the British camp.

On October 14, Washington gave the order. The soldiers would attack the last two redoubts at night. Washington did not want his men accidentally shooting their comrades in the dark so he ordered them not to load their muskets. This strike would be with bayonets only.

WORDS TO KNOW

redoubt: a temporary fortification.

duel: a fight between two people with weapons, in front of witnesses.

DID YOU KNOW?

Alexander Hamilton led the assault on Redoubt 10. He was born into poverty on a Caribbean island and migrated to America. During the war, Hamilton became one of General Washington's favorite aides. Hamilton later served as the first secretary of the treasury for the United States. He was killed in a duel with Vice President Aaron Burr in 1804.

99

The sappers went first. These were men with axes to chop through the wooden spikes that defended the redoubts. When the time came to charge the redoubts, soldiers whispered the code word up and down their line—"Rochambeau."

Joseph Plumb Martin, a soldier in the army who later wrote about his experience, thought that this was a good code. "Our watchword was 'Rochambeau,'" he wrote. ". . . a good watchword, for being pronounced Ro-sham-bow, it sounded, when pronounced quick, like rush-on-boys." And rush on they did. Within 15 minutes, the American and French soldiers captured both redoubts.

Howitzers and cannons were dragged into these strongholds, and the next morning the British woke to blistering fire.

Cornwallis was desperate. The night of October 16, he tried to ferry his army across the York River, hoping to flee north. But Cornwallis was having terrible luck—a storm rose up and he had to return to camp.

Surrender Ceremony

In the eighteenth century, it was tradition for a defeated commander to surrender his sword to the victorious commander. When the British surrendered at Yorktown, General Cornwallis claimed he was too sick to attend the ceremony. The British second-in-command, Brigadier General Charles O'Hara, attended the ceremony instead. He tried to hand his sword to General Rochambeau, implying that the victory belonged to the French, not the Americans. Rochambeau refused to accept the sword and pointed to General Washington. But Washington refused to accept the sword from anyone other than Cornwallis. Finally, Washington's second-in-command, General Benjamin Lincoln, took the sword from O'Hara. Why did Washington insist on following tradition?

On October 17, 1781, a red-coated soldier beat a drum as he climbed the last remaining British fortification. The French and American guns fell silent.

A British officer appeared, waving a white flag. Cornwallis had surrendered.

Treaty of Paris

When news of the victory at Yorktown spread through America, people celebrated! No one thought the war was over—and technically it wasn't. Fighting between Native Americans and Americans continued on the frontier. Small fights between patriots and loyalists broke out in New York, New Jersey, and the Carolinas. But the Battle of Yorktown was the last major military engagement between the British and Continental armies.

Parliament knew it needed the 30,000 British troops that still remained in America after Yorktown to protect other areas of the British Empire. France, Spain, and Holland had their eyes on British lands in the Caribbean and Africa. With British citizens sick of the high price of war, British officials finally agreed to talk peace.

In 1782, Great Britain gave America what it had long wanted. The British government formally stated that the United States was an independent nation.

?

THESIS STATEMENT

Now it's time to interpret what you have read in this chapter and answer the Essential Question:

How did General Washington's decision to march his army to Yorktown affect the outcome of the war? Do you consider him a good general?

ACTIVITY

Build Your Own Redoubt

Supplies: *empty box, scissors, blue construction paper, dirt, glue, paints, paintbrush, floral Styrofoam, dull knife, twigs, toothpicks, empty spool of thread, eraser and metal end of a wooden pencil*

Eighteenth-century technology was basic—shovels, sticks, and dirt. This was what British soldiers used to build their redoubts in Yorktown. You probably aren't facing an enemy attack, but if you were, what would you use to build a redoubt to give yourself the best chance for success? The supplies listed above can be used to build a small model of a redoubt, or you can think of your own materials. Are you going to build a tabletop model or a larger redoubt in your yard? Can you use your couch, chairs, pillows, and blankets to build a redoubt in your living room?

Each redoubt had several basic parts to it:

* ★ **parapet:** the mound of dirt around a redoubt
* ★ **banquette:** a flat part behind the parapet where British soldiers stood to fire over the parapet
* ★ **scarp:** the side of the ditch leading up to the parapet
* ★ **ditch:** a long trench dug in front of the parapet
* ★ **palisade:** a fence made of pointed sticks stuck in the bottom of the ditch
* ★ **abatis:** a row of sharpened sticks stuck in the sides of the scarps to catch attacking soldiers

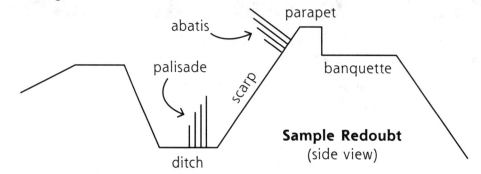

Sample Redoubt
(side view)

1 Paint a background battle scene on your paper and then glue the paper all around the walls inside the box to create your scene. Fill your box about halfway with dirt, and dig a ditch across the box.

2 Cut a rectangle and a half circle from the Styrofoam to create the parapet and the banquette, where the British soldiers stand and fire their artillery at the advancing Continental Army. Bury your parapet enough so it stands on its own next to the ditch. Can you imagine colonial soldiers trying to climb the steep scarp while British soldiers fire on them from the banquette?

3 Poke the twigs into the dirt in a straight line at the bottom of the ditch to make the palisade. Use the toothpicks to make an abatis at the top of the parapet. The abatis is used in the same way barbed wire is used now. Do you think it works as well?

4 Paint the spool and pencil end black and glue the pencil to the top of the spool. Glue your cannon to the top of the banquette, facing it toward the ditch so it can fire on attacking enemies.

THINK MORE: Redoubts have been used in many wars, both before and after the American Revolution. However, as armies became more mobile with tanks and armored vehicles, redoubts have not been used as much. Why does a mobile army have less need for a redoubt? What might a mobile army need instead?

ACTIVITY

Make Your Own Military Analysis

Supplies: *Historical Detective Journal, map of Siege of Yorktown, pen, computer with Internet access*

What were the essential factors that led to the defeat of Cornwallis's forces at the Battle of Yorktown? Perform an analysis of the battle to answer this question.

1 On a blank page in your history journal draw a table with two columns labeled "Advantages" and "Disadvantages."

2 Draw four rows across this table and label them: "Armies of Washington & Rochambeau," "French Navy," "British Navy," and "Army of Cornwallis."

	Advantages	Disadvantages
Armies of Washington & Rochambeau		
French Navy		
British Navy		
Army of Cornwallis		

3 With an adult's permission, research online to find a map of the Battle of Yorktown. Use information from the map and the description of the battle from the text to record the advantages and disadvantages that each group faced during this battle.

4 Consider your evidence and answer this question: What was the essential factor that led to Cornwallis's defeat at the Battle of Yorktown? Write your answer in your journal.

DID YOU KNOW?

★ ★ ★ ★ ★ ★ ★ ★ ★ ★

General Washington created a "Badge for Military Merit" made out of purple cloth and shaped like a heart. Today this medal is called the Purple Heart. It's awarded to individuals who have been wounded in action.

Chapter 8
The Promise of Peace

Spring in Philadelphia in May 1787 was a time of hope
and renewal, and a time to get to work. The leaders
of the newly born United States were back at the
Pennsylvania State House. The war with Great Britain had
been over for more than three years, but the struggle
to create a workable government had just begun.

demigod: a mythical being with more power than a human but less than a god.

pardon: to forgive.

WORDS TO KNOW

Fresh dirt had been laid down on the cobblestone street in front of the State House to muffle the clatter of the wheels of passing carriages. Guards stood by the doors of the building to prevent any curiosity seekers from trying to enter. The men inside the State House were the celebrities of the time—Thomas Jefferson even described them as **demigods**. The most famed of those men, George Washington, was elected president of the Constitutional Convention. What lay before the leaders was a weighty task—the very salvation of a fragile nation.

DID YOU KNOW?

In 1787 citizens took up arms against the new government. Veteran Daniel Shays led an army of desperate farmers in an attack on a courthouse in Massachusetts. The rebels were arrested and convicted but later **pardoned.** Shays's Rebellion was proof that the Articles of Confederation were not working.

The Articles of Confederation

In 1781, while the war still raged, the Continental Congress created a new government. It was based on a document called the Articles of Confederation. This government set up a "league of friendship" between the 13 states. Members of Congress were determined to never be ruled by a distant government again, but the Articles of Confederation did not supply the new government with the tools to govern.

The Articles of Confederation described a Confederation Congress. Each state had one vote in this law-making body. Technically, the Confederation Congress could negotiate with foreign countries. It could also regulate currency and go to war.

In reality, the Congress was powerless. It was not allowed to tax citizens, and a government without money cannot govern.

? ESSENTIAL QUESTION

How was compromise important to the final Constitution that the Founding Fathers wrote?

foreclose: to take possession of someone's property when he or she cannot pay the debt on it.

WORDS TO KNOW

After the war, life did not go well for the United States under the Articles of Confederation. American ships had no navy to protect them and were often seized by Caribbean pirates. Native Americans violently resisted colonial settlements in the Ohio River Valley, and Congress had no army to patrol this land to keep the peace. Great Britain closed off its Caribbean ports to American trade. Spain refused to let American boats use the Mississippi River to get to the port of New Orleans. Crop prices fell. Farmers could not pay their bills and banks began to **foreclose** on their lands.

The United States was also in serious debt. It owed $7.9 million to France and the Netherlands. Congress also owed more than $34 million to citizens who had loaned the government money during the war. Veterans of the Continental Army had fought without pay for years and needed to be paid too. Each state began to issue its own paper currency. This money quickly became worthless and prices skyrocketed. In some areas, a pound of tea cost $100.

By 1787 the United States was on the verge of collapse. In desperation, political leaders called a meeting of representatives from all 13 states. This meeting was called the Constitutional Convention, and its purpose was to repair the Articles of Confederation.

Constitutional Convention

Delegates to the Constitutional Convention quickly realized there was no way to fix the Articles of Confederation. They needed to start from scratch. Through the humid summer, 55 delegates worked to create an entirely new national government.

Luckily, James Madison had come to the Constitutional Convention with a plan. This delegate from Virginia had studied government and legal theories and devised a proposal for a new government. It would be strong enough to rule all 13 states but free enough to avoid tyranny. Madison did not miss a single day of the convention. He took detailed notes of every meeting. He later said the summer almost killed him.

The main issue that posed problems for the delegates was how many votes each state should have in a new congress. Should each state get one vote regardless of population? Small states, such as New Jersey, said yes. States with large populations, including Virginia, disagreed.

DID YOU KNOW?

George Washington was not the first president of the United States. That title belongs to John Hanson, the first president under the Articles of Confederation. However, this position had no real power and was eliminated when a new system of government was created in 1787.

If a state's representatives depended on population, how should slaves be counted? States with few slaves, such as Massachusetts, believed that slaves should not be included in the population count. After all, slaves were not allowed to vote. States with large slave populations, such as South Carolina, refused to accept any national government that restricted slavery. The convention was on the verge of collapse.

The heat in the Philadelphia statehouse was intense. Bluebottle flies buzzed around the delegates' heads and tempers flared. But a compromise was found.

On September 17, 1787, the document called the Constitution was signed.

The Constitution

The Constitution created a strong national government with three branches. The executive branch includes the president, the vice president, and a group of advisors called the cabinet. This branch enforces the laws. The first president under the Constitution was George Washington.

Read the Constitution

The Constitution might be the most important document in U.S. history. **Read it for yourself.** How did the Founding Fathers make it possible for the country to adapt to a future its citizens couldn't know?

WORDS TO KNOW

veto: an official vote of "no" from the person in power.

Congress makes up the legislative branch and is responsible for making the laws. Two bodies of Congress share this power: the Senate and the House of Representatives. Each state elects two senators. The number of representatives each state has in the house depends on its population. This was the compromise reached between the big and small states.

The third branch of government under the Constitution is the judicial branch. This branch is made up of the federal courts. Their job is to interpret the laws to make sure they follow the Constitution. The highest court in the land is the Supreme Court. It is made up of nine people who are the final judges of whether or not a law violates the Constitution.

DID YOU KNOW?

At the Constitutional Convention, Alexander Hamilton proposed that the country have a leader who would serve for life with complete veto power. He was basically proposing that the United States have a king!

The system of government created by the Constitution is called a republic. The people exercise power by voting for representatives to rule for them.

Republic Government		
Branch	Made up of	Job
executive	president, vice president, advisors (cabinet)	enforces the laws
legislative	congress (senate and house of representatives)	makes the laws
judicial	federal courts	interprets the laws

The delegates compromised on slavery by deciding that a slave would count for three-fifths of a person when it came to determining how many representatives a state had in the House of Representatives. If a man from Virginia owned 100 slaves, he actually counted as 61 people in terms of Virginia's population.

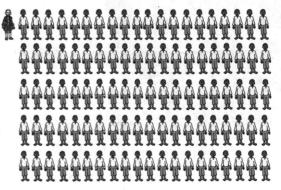

100 slaves = 60 citizens

This solution was called the Three-Fifths Compromise. The Constitution laid out freedoms for whites but kept shackles on slaves. These divisions regarding slavery would eventually erupt into the American Civil War in the 1860s.

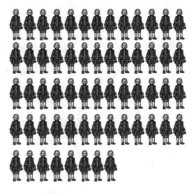

Ratification

The Constitution had to be **ratified** by at least nine of the 13 states before it could become law. Two camps emerged: Federalists supported the Constitution because they wanted a strong national government, but Anti-federalists feared a government that was too strong would trample on peoples' liberties. The debate raged in taverns, on street corners, and in the newspapers. Five of the 13 states ratified the Constitution quickly, but the rest hesitated.

In February 1788, another compromise was reached. Anti-federalists agreed to ratify the Constitution as long as a "bill of rights" was added to it. They believed that this would protect citizens from a national government that might try to take their liberties away. In June 1788, New Hampshire became the ninth state to ratify the Constitution. It was now the law of the land.

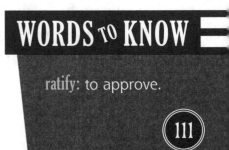

WORDS TO KNOW

ratify: to approve.

111

After the Constitution was written and ratified, it was amended. To amend something is to change it. The first 10 **amendments** to the Constitution are the Bill of Rights.

These amendments limit the government's power. For example, the First Amendment gives people freedom of religion, freedom of the press, freedom of speech, the right to gather peacefully, and the right to ask their government to fix problems. That's five liberties protected in just one amendment!

The freedoms preserved in the Bill of Rights represent the values of the people of the United States.

Legacies of the Revolutionary War

The revolution was partly a war to protect wealth and property. Americans rebelled when the British tried to control their trade and take their money in the form of taxes.

In the eighteenth century, slaves were considered property. The revolution defined the United States as a slave nation. However, the Declaration of Independence instilled the values of liberty and equality into the American soul. White people began to struggle with the contradiction between viewing slaves as property and their ideas of equality. By the end of the war, all Northern states had laws that gradually ended slavery. But it would take a civil war before the Thirteenth Amendment was added to the Constitution to ban slavery everywhere in the United States for all time.

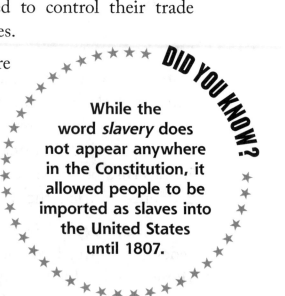

DID YOU KNOW?

While the word *slavery* does not appear anywhere in the Constitution, it allowed people to be imported as slaves into the United States until 1807.

Women were treated as second-class citizens in the United States. They could not vote, attend college, or become doctors, lawyers, or ministers. However, the revolution did raise public awareness of the roles of women. The new nation needed good leaders, and women were assigned the new title of Republican Mothers.

Many women took seriously this patriotic duty to raise smart, hard-working sons to lead the United States to greatness.

However, other women wanted more from life than motherhood. They wanted the full promise of life, liberty, and the pursuit of happiness. Women knew they would never achieve these rights if they could not vote. For more than 100 years, women marched, went on hunger strikes, and even went to jail as they fought for the right to vote.

Finally, in 1920, the Nineteenth Amendment was ratified. This constitutional amendment says the right to vote cannot be denied because of a person's sex.

Women at the Polls

The struggle for equal rights for women continues today. Though women do have the right to vote and run for elected positions, no woman has ever been president. Women hold 19 percent of the seats in Congress, 20 percent of the seats in the Senate and 18 percent of the seats in the House of Representatives.

You can look at photographs of women protesting for women's rights. Do you think your life would be different if women hadn't won the right to vote?

The end of the Revolutionary War marked the beginning of a series of battles between the United States government and Native Americans. These small-scale, bloody wars lasted until the end of the nineteenth century. The U.S. government eventually signed treaties with the tribes, although it repeatedly broke the promises made in these agreements. Finally, near the end of the twentieth century, Native American people sued in court to have the treaties upheld.

Today, more than 192 countries have declarations of independence among their founding documents. These declarations were made in different centuries, on different continents, by different cultures. When people believe their government is unjust, they rise up to protect their liberties. Can you think of countries today where the people are following the example of the United States and taking action to demand a government of representation?

DID YOU KNOW?

The Constitution has been amended 27 times. The last amendment was in 1992 and it dealt with the pay of members of Congress.

? THESIS STATEMENT

Now it's time to interpret what you have read in this chapter and answer the Essential Question:

How was compromise important to the final Constitution that the Founding Fathers wrote?

ACTIVITY

Write Your Own Bill of Rights

Supplies: *several friends, paper, colored pencils, quill pen from activity on page 67*

The Bill of Rights was created to ensure that Americans remained free from a government that was too strong. If you were writing a bill of rights for your own society, what would you include? Would it be different from the Bill of Rights for the United States? Read the original Bill of Rights here.

1 Along with a group of friends, draw pictures of the rights you think are the most important. How are these different from the rights guaranteed in the original Bill of Rights? Are any the same?

2 Work with your friends to choose 10 freedoms to include in your own bill of rights. Write them up on a clean piece of paper and have everyone sign it with a quill pen.

TRY THIS: Think about what your life will be like in another 20 years. Do you think your bill of rights will still apply? What might you want to add or take away?

ACTIVITY

Make Your Own "We the People" Flag

Supplies: *white poster board, paint (red, white, and blue), paintbrush, old magazines, scissors, glue stick*

During the last two centuries, the concept of citizenship in the United States has expanded. Create a flag that represents what it means to be an American in the twenty-first century.

1 Paint a blue square in the upper left corner of the poster board and seven red stripes in the remaining white section.

2 When the blue paint is dry, use the paintbrush or your fingertip to make 50 white dots (stars) in the blue square. What do these white dots represent?

3 Page through the magazines while you think about what it means to be an American today. Consider your classmates, friends, neighbors, teachers, and leaders. What do they look like? What do they care about? Cut out images and words that represent "We the People" today. Glue these words and images over your flag.

TRY THIS: What if you made a flag like this right after the Revolutionary War? How many stars would it have? Would the two flags look different in other ways? How?

accurate: true, correct.

adapt: to make a change in response to new or different conditions.

allied: joined together.

amendment: a correction, addition, or change to the U.S. constitution.

American Revolution: the war between the colonies and England from 1775 to 1783 that ended with the creation of the independent United States of America.

barracks: housing for soldiers.

barter: to trade goods without relying on money.

bayonet: a sword-like blade fixed to the end of a gun for hand-to-hand fighting.

boycott: refusing to buy or use a product.

British: citizens of the kingdom of Great Britain, which consisted of England, Scotland, and Wales.

bumpkin: an awkward, simple person; today we would say hick or redneck.

Christopher Columbus: an Italian explorer who landed in the Americas while seeking a route to China.

citizen: a person who has all the rights and responsibilities that come with being a full member of a country.

civil disobedience: refusing to obey certain laws or pay taxes as a peaceful form of political protest.

colonial: relating to the years 1607 through 1776, when people from Europe settled in colonies in America—which eventually became the United States of America.

colony: a territory controlled by another country.

commons: an area of land in colonial America shared by a community for grazing animals.

company: the military name for a group of soldiers that trains and fights together.

compromise: an agreement made when each side gives in a little.

conservative: someone who is cautious about change.

crop: a plant grown for food and other uses.

currency: a system of money.

customs agent: a government official who collects taxes on imports and exports.

debt: an amount of money or something else that is owed.

delegate: someone sent to a meeting to represent others.

demigod: a mythical being with more power than a human but less than a god.

democracy: a system of government where the people choose who will represent and govern them.

disperse: to scatter over a wide area.

draft: a government requirement that men join the military.

duel: a fight between two people with weapons, in front of witnesses.

economy: the wealth and resources of an area or country.

effigy: a fake model of a person.

eloquently: using language clearly and effectively, showing feeling and meaning.

empire: a group of countries controlled by one government.

endowed: to be given something.

endure: to experience for a long time.

enforce: to carry out a law.

enlist: to voluntarily join the military.

equality: being treated the same, with the same rights and opportunities as others.

evidence: facts or arguments that prove a case.

execute: to put to death.

export: to send goods to another country to sell.

express rider: someone who carried messages from town to town on horseback.

fertile: good for growing crops.

fife: a wooden flute with six finger holes.

First Congressional Congress: delegates from each colony except Georgia who met to discuss the colonies' reaction to Britain.

foreclose: to take possession of someone's property when he or she cannot pay the debt on it.

fortification: a walled-in area to protect against an enemy.

Founding Fathers: members of the Constitutional Convention who founded the United States.

goods: items that can be bought, sold, or traded.

gun carriage: the platform that carries a cannon.

Hessian: a professional German soldier hired by the British Army.

historian: a person who investigates events and people of the past.

immigrant: a person who leaves his or her own country to live in another country.

import: to bring a product into a country to be sold.

indigo: a plant used to make dark blue dyes.

GLOSSARY

inflation: a continuing rise in the price of goods and services.

interpret: to think about something and explain it.

jury trial: a meeting in court before a judge and a group of people called a jury where evidence about a crime or disagreement is presented and decisions are made according to the law.

King George III: the leader of Great Britain.

legislative assembly: the group within the government that makes laws.

liberty: freedom from too much control by the government.

liberty pole: a tall wooden pole put up in many colonial towns. When a red cap was hung from the pole, people gathered to protest British laws.

limited monarchy: a government in which a king's power is limited by laws.

livestock: animals raised for food and other uses.

longboat: a large boat used to carry soldiers from ship to shore.

massacre: the deliberate killing of many people.

meetinghouse: a building used for public meetings and as a church.

mercantilism: an economic system whose goal is to hold as much wealth in gold and silver as possible. To do this a nation needs to export more products than it imports. Britain's colonies were both suppliers of its imports and a market for its exports.

merchant: a person who buys and sells goods for a profit.

militia: an army made up of citizens instead of professional soldiers.

minutemen: a special group of colonial militia who were ready to fight in a minute's notice.

Mohawk: a tribe of Native Americans, part of the Iroquois Confederacy.

monopoly: when one company has complete control over trade of an area or product.

morale: feelings of enthusiasm and loyalty that a person or group has about a task or job.

mother country: the country that a person or group of people comes from.

musket ball: ammunition fired by muskets, a type of long gun used by soldiers before the invention of rifles.

mutiny: a rebellion of soldiers against their commanding officer.

nation: another word for country.

New England: the Northeastern colonies of Massachusetts, Connecticut, New Hampshire, and Rhode Island. Today New England also includes the states of Maine and Vermont.

New World: what is now America. It was called the New World by people from Europe because it was new to them.

nonviolent: characterized by not using physical force or power.

North America: the continent that includes the United States, Canada, Mexico, and all of the countries of Central America and the Caribbean.

pardon: to forgive.

Parliament: the law-making body of British government.

patriot: in colonial America, someone who resisted British rule. The British called these people rebels.

patrol: to keep watch over an area.

pension: an amount of money paid at regular times for past service.

petition: a formal, written request.

plantation: a large farm in a hot climate. In colonial times, plantations used slaves as workers.

poverty: the state of being very poor.

power: a person, group, or country that is stronger than others.

preamble: an introduction.

principle: an important idea or belief that guides an individual or community.

privateer: a privately owned ship that the government paid to capture enemy vessels.

proclamation: a public announcement.

profit: the money made by selling an item or service for more than it cost.

propaganda: the use of information, often false or exaggerated, to persuade people.

protest: to object to something, often in public.

pursuit: to try to catch something.

rallying: causing a group of people to have new energy and enthusiasm for something.

ransack: to search for something in a way that causes damage or makes a mess.

ratify: to approve.

rebel: someone fighting against authority.

rebellion: an organized attempt to overthrow a government or other authority.

redcoat: slang for British soldiers, whose uniforms included red jackets.

redoubt: a temporary fortification.

regiment: a unit of soldiers.

reinforcements: more troops.

repeal: to withdraw.

resolution: a firm decision to do or not do something.

retreat: to move away from the enemy in battle.

revolt: to fight against a government or person of authority.

revolution: an attempt to overthrow a government and replace it with a new system.

right: something that a person is or should be allowed to have, get, or do.

riot: a gathering of people protesting something, which gets out of control and violent.

Second Continental Congress: delegates from the colonies who met in 1775 to discuss whether or not America should declare its independence.

shackle: to chain a prisoner's wrists or ankles together.

siege: when the military surrounds a town or enemy fort and does not allow anything in or out.

slang: a nickname for something, used mostly in speech.

slogan: a phrase used by a business or other group to get attention.

smuggle: to move goods illegally in or out of a country.

stalemate: a contest where neither side is winning.

stanza: a group of lines that form a part of a poem.

tar and feather: a form of punishment where hot tar is smeared over a person's body and then feathers are poured over him.

tax: an extra charge the government adds to the price of goods and services.

thesis statement: the main point or main conclusion a historian makes after researching a specific question.

traitor: someone who is disloyal and abandons or betrays a group or cause.

treason: actions that go against one's own country.

treaty: a written agreement between two countries.

tyranny: cruel and unfair treatment by people in power.

tyrant: a cruel ruler who denies people their rights.

unalienable: something that cannot be taken away.

value: a strongly held belief about what is valuable, important, or acceptable.

veto: an official vote of "no" from the person in power.

volley: many bullets fired at once.

Yankee Doodle: slang used by the British to ridicule someone from New England.

Metric Equivalents

Use this chart to find the metric equivalents to the English measurements in this book. If you need to know a half measurement, divide by two. If you need to know twice the measurement, multiply by two. How do you find a quarter measurement? How do you find three times the measurement?

English	Metric
1 inch	2.5 centimeters
1 foot	30.5 centimeters
1 yard	0.9 meters
1 mile	1.6 kilometers
1 pound	0.5 kilogram
1 teaspoon	5 milliliters
1 tablespoon	15 milliliters
1 cup	237 milliliters

RESOURCES

Websites

Liberty! The American Revolution: *pbs.org/ktca/liberty/chronicle.html*

Games & Activities: *history.org/kids/games/index.cfm*

National Park Service Museum Collections:
cr.nps.gov/museum/exhibits/revwar/index1.html

Facts about Washington and his World: *mountvernon.org/students*

Spy Letters of the American Revolution:
clements.umich.edu/exhibits/online/spies/index-main2.html

Museums, Monuments, and Sites to Visit

Colonial Williamsburg, Virginia: *colonialwilliamsburg.com/discover*

Independence Hall National Historical Park, Pennsylvania:
nps.gov/inde/index.htm

Valley Forge National Historical Park, Pennsylvania: *nps.gov/vafo/index.htm*

Minute Man National Historical Park, Massachusetts: *nps.gov/mima/index.htm*

Freedom Trail, Massachusetts: *thefreedomtrail.org/freedom-trail/index.shtml*

Yorktown Battlefield, Yorktown, Virginia: *nps.gov/york/index.htm*

Mount Vernon, Virginia: *mountvernon.org*

Saratoga National Historical Park, New York: *nps.gov/sara/index.htm*

QR Code Glossary

Page 2: *loc.gov/resource/g3300.ar004200*

Page 6: *masshist.org/database/viewer.php?item_id=98&img_step=1&mode=dual#page1*

Page 15: *poetryfoundation.org/poem/175140*

Page 25: *gutenberg.org/files/15399/15399-h/15399-h.htm#CHAP_II*

Page 40: *smithsoniansource.org/display/primarysource/viewdetails. aspx?PrimarySourceId=1074*

Page 44: *paul-revere-heritage.com/boston-massacre-engraving.html*

Page 59: *en.wikipedia.org/wiki/Dunmore%27s_Proclamation#mediaviewer/ File:DunmoresProclamation.jpg*

Page 63: *archives.gov/exhibits/charters/declaration_transcript.html*

Page 71: *en.wikipedia.org/wiki/Washington_Crossing_the_Delaware#mediaviewer/ File:Washington_Crossing_the_Delaware_by_Emanuel_Leutze,_MMA-NYC,_1851.jpg*

Page 79: *mountvernon.org/george-washington/the-revolutionary-war/george-washington- spymaster/the-culper-code-book*

Page 109: *usconstitution.cc*

Page 109: *workhousemuseums.org/index.php?option=com_ wrapper&view=wrapper&Itemid=6*

Page 115: *billofrightsinstitute.org/wp-content/uploads/2011/12/BillofRights.pdf*